BAIL BONDS 101

BAIL BONDS 101

The Complete Guide to Owning and Operating a Successful Bail Bond Company

Sean M. Cook

ISBN 0-9764958-0-5
Bail Out Publishing, Huntington Beach CA

Thank you to everyone

who helped me create a successful bail bond business.

CONTENTS

BAIL BONDS 101

INTRODUCTION

If you were to ask someone what bail agents do, that person would probably frown and say, "They let criminals out of jail." You could argue that an attorney does the same thing. But if you were to ask what attorneys do, the response would probably be, "They represent you in court." The bail agent has struggled against this negative image since the industry began. The media has portrayed bail agents as sleazy men in greasy shirts or villainous men who smoke cigars and threaten to break other people's kneecaps.

In the past, some of these scenarios may have been true. There were bail agents that let hookers out of jail in exchange for sex, or dealers out of jail in exchange for drugs. Some bail agents were criminals themselves. But this is all in the past.

There's a new face to the bail agent. The modern bail agent wears a suit and treats his job as a business. Many young second- and third-generation bond agents are joining their family businesses and bringing in fresh ideas and a new approach. As a result, the bail bond industry has changed into a reputable and rewarding business. Over 10,000 people across the United States earn their living as bail agents.

This book gives you the details you need to better

understand the inner workings of the bail industry, from its history to the nuts and bolts of starting your own bail bond business. The book is written from the point of view of a bail agent in California. However, most of the issues addressed are common to many states. To find out the specifics for your state, contact the state agency that regulates the bail bond industry. In most states, it's the Department of Insurance, but in other states this responsibility falls under the Department of Commerce or a similar department. Links to the appropriate agencies in all 50 states appear in *Appendix – Resources*.

While the pronoun "he" is used for convenience in this book to refer to bail agents, keep in mind that many women earn their living as bail agents. Often they perform their job better than men.

People are arrested every day across the United States. With this book and some determination, you can soon be providing them with a valuable service protected by the 8th Amendment to the United States Constitution. You can become a successful bail agent.

1

AN OVERVIEW OF BAIL BONDING

Why should you become a bail agent? At first glance, it seems there are more reasons *not* to become part of the bail industry: The job is misunderstood, the hours are irregular, the financial risk can be high, and the industry is still struggling for prestige. However, the job provides many benefits:

- Quick financial gain: Depending on the state, just one simple domestic violence case can earn the bail agent $2,500 to $5,000. In Los Angeles, California, for example, the bail agent can earn an immediate $5,000 on a domestic violence case, and the time required to post this type of bond can be as little as 15 minutes or at most a few days, depending on the situation.
- Community service: Bail agents provide a valuable service. Without the bail system, citizens facing

possible prosecution would be trapped in jail, even if charged with a minor crime or even if they are innocent. Like all legal systems, the bail industry exists to protect the innocent. Bail agents make a positive contribution to society by ensuring this system works.

- Interesting atmosphere: Bail agents handle different types of cases every day. They work closely with law enforcement agencies, from local police to U.S. marshals. They appear in courts and interact with attorneys, judges, district attorneys, public defenders, and other legal industry professionals. Bail agents are at the center of the fascinating world of criminal justice.

Bail agents play a unique role in our court system. If the criminal justice system were a game of football, the bail agent would be on special teams. The agent's work supports both the offense and the defense. He is a vital player for both sides of the system.

On one side are the individuals suspected of crimes. Once they are arrested, they are confined to jail. This makes sense if they are guilty. But what if they are innocent? An individual's right to personal liberty is one of our most basic rights. When individuals are detained in jail, the bail agent helps them protect their right to personal freedom as they defend themselves in court.

On the other side is the court system, which upholds society's need to enforce laws and seek justice against someone who has committed a crime. In his role on this side of the system, the bail agent guarantees that the defendant will appear in court and, if not, he will pay the full amount of the defendant's bail. The guarantee of a court appearance is critical. The criminal justice system fails if, when a case has come before the court, the prosecutor is ready to try the case, the witnesses have left their jobs in order to testify, the judge is on the bench, the jury has been seated, the prosecutor is ready to make his motions, as is the defense – and no defendant is available to be tried.

Misconceptions

Bail agents help protect the rights of individuals and preserve the justice provided by our court system, which helps protect society. All of this sounds very noble, but still the negative image of bail agents persists. Most people know about bail agents only through fictionalized television shows and movies that focus on negative aspects of the bail industry.

Many misconceptions result:

1. Bail agents help hardened criminals elude justice

Actually, most cases handled by bail agents involve average citizens who used poor judgment at the wrong time, possibly for the first time. A normally law-abiding citizen suddenly finds himself in jail and is probably unfamiliar with the inner workings of the U.S. criminal justice system. Helping this individual protect his rights and gain freedom, if only temporarily, is rewarding. Bail agents provide one of the most important services these people will ever need.

It's true that hardened criminals are entitled to the same services, but in most cases they will be denied bail by the court. Then there are the cases in which someone accused of a violent crime might actually be innocent. Approximately one-third of the defendants facing felony charges are not convicted.

2. Bail agents are shifty, shady people

Bail agents are often found guilty by association. People think that a bail agent represents the defendant or is somehow proclaiming the defendant to be innocent by releasing him from jail. This is a misconception. The bail agent is simply helping the defendant protect his constitutionally given right to be released while he awaits trial.

This misconception is reinforced when a high-profile defendant is released on bail. In such a case, it's easy for the public to believe the bail agent is shady. They see him as instrumental in releasing a person already found guilty in the public eye. Remember that it's not up to the public or the bail agent to determine a person's innocence or guilt. That's up to the jury.

Of course, some of the defendants released on bail will be found guilty by a jury. When law enforcement agents spend hours investigating a crime and tracking down the perpetrator, it's understandable that they want to see him locked up. Imagine their frustration when a bail agent lets that suspected criminal walk away from jail – particularly because they remember past cases in which a defendant skipped town while on bail and was never brought to justice.

A guilty person skipping town is an unfortunate cost of our effort to maintain a fair justice system. But it's a necessary cost. We can't detain all defendants in jail simply to prevent a few from escaping justice. Unfortunately the frustration at seeing a potentially guilty criminal walk free adds to the misconceptions of the bail agent's role.

Nor is the bail agent's image helped when people see his name posted on flyers, billboards and bus benches near jails and in inner-city areas where crime rates are higher. When people see a bail agent's ad posted in these areas, they perceive that he is involved with criminal elements. They don't realize that such advertisements are honest ways to promote the bail agent's legitimate services. The bail agent isn't doing anything wrong. His services are a crucial and legal part of the criminal justice system.

3. Bail agents are not professionals

A bail agent is a professional in the criminal justice system. Unfortunately, the bail agent's professional image is countered by the negative stereotypes portrayed on television, along with the real-life misdeeds of some bail agents in the past. In many people's minds, the bail agent's job description comes down to one sentence: "Bail agents get you out of jail for money."

The industry has been working to establish itself as a professional trade to gain the respect it is due. Bail agents have formed national, state and local bail associations to promote the proper image and give all agents a voice in improving the industry. Industry trade shows provide educational workshops and keep the bail agent's knowledge up to date.

It might surprise some people to learn that bail agents attend educational workshops. A common misconception is that education plays no role in the bail bond industry. Just because no university major is offered in bail bonding doesn't mean a bail agent isn't educated or lacks the character and standards of other professionals.

Modern bail agents are certified through training courses. In most states, they are required to pass an exam in order to be licensed. Most states also require that bail agents take continuing education classes in order to renew their licenses and improve their professional status.

4. Bail agents always have rolls of cash in their pockets

Do you see attorneys carrying around the cash they earned? Not usually. Why should bail agents be expected to carry rolls of cash in their pockets?

As with any other business professional, the bail agent deposits the fees he earns straight into his bank account. While it's true that a defendant can pay his bond with a roll of cash, that's a rare occurrence. If a bail agent's fee is paid in cash, he is anxious to deposit the money into his bank account as quickly as possible. He doesn't want to carry it around.

Aside from his fees earned, the rest of the money accumulated by the bail agent is simply collateral (*see Chapter 4 – How Bail Works*). Collateral is anything of value that can be used as security for the bail bond – something worth as much as the full amount of bail. While most collateral is in the form of real estate or other property, sometimes cash collateral is offered.

Cash collateral is kept in a trust account while the defendant appears in court. As long as the defendant makes all of his court appearances throughout the duration of his case, the cash collateral will be returned to him. When a bail agent accepts cash collateral, the bail payment to the court isn't made with that cash but is deposited in the form of a bond, which is a piece of paper that represents cash – similar in concept to a check. This bond guarantees the court will receive the bail if the defendant fails to appear.

5. Bail agents spend most of their time hanging around jails

Very little of the bail agent's time is spent at the jail. Most paperwork is completed at the agent's office. Unless the agent has a bad sense of décor, the atmosphere is not unpleasant. People cosigning the bond can meet at the bail agent's office to sign the required paperwork. Even if the bail agent meets with the cosigner at the jail, the time spent there is minimal, because the paperwork has been prepared in advance.

By the time they meet, the bail agent and the cosigner will already have come to an agreement by phone and made arrangements to post bail. While waiting for the cosigner to arrive, the agent has time to prepare the paperwork so that the process can be expedited and the cosigner will not have to wait long. In most cases, a few minutes, a few signatures, and the defendant is released from jail.

Some of the larger jails and police departments can take up to several hours to release a defendant after posting bail. Most often the bail agent will not wait around for the defendant to be released. He will require the defendant to visit his office to complete paperwork pertaining to his bail.

6. Bail agents are greedy and will do anything for money

The bail agent is ultimately liable to the courts for the full amount of bail. He certainly doesn't want to have to pay the entire bail amount. Therefore he's careful to ensure that the defendant is reliable and will make the scheduled court appearances. Many bail agents turn down clients if they believe the defendant is going to skip bail or just have a bad feeling about the situation.

Bail agents are like any other business professional: They are in business to earn a living. This doesn't mean they will do anything for a fee, because ultimately the responsibility to the court falls on the bail agent. As long as the bail agent carefully screens defendants and does not get greedy when bailing people out of jail, his business will succeed. Bail agents are very smart and have a good sense about people. In most cases, they know right away when someone is trying to deceive them.

7. Bail agents keep people's houses, cars, boats and jewelry

Rarely is a bail agent required to keep or foreclose on the property of a client. This happens only in extreme cases when a cosigner is not cooperating and doesn't care about the collateral he used to guarantee the defendant's appearance in court.

In most cases, the defendant has been carefully screened. Bail agents are business professionals and they have to keep the bottom line in sight. They can't pay their mortgage with a boat. They can't pay their utilities bill with a car title. They aren't in the business of repossessing assets and don't have time to try and sell the items given to them as collateral. That would leave little or no time to promote their businesses and attend to new clients.

Moreover, the bail agent has no right to foreclose on a house posted as collateral unless the defendant doesn't show up for his court appearance and all other avenues have been exhausted. The responsibility there lies with the defendant, who has been told in advance that his house – or his best friend's house – will be confiscated if he does not appear in court. Even when a defendant fails to appear in court and cannot be located, most cosigners will find a way to pay off the bond rather than allowing their house to go into foreclosure.

Why do people need bail agents?

With the negative misconceptions out of the way, we can examine how bail agents really work and what it will take for you to establish a successful bail bond agency.

Why does a person go to a bail agent? Bail agents exist because most people can't afford to pay the full amount of bail or don't want to part with that much money. For example, if a defendant's bail amount is $25,000 and the bail is handled by a bail agent, the cosigner will need to come up with only 10%, or $2,500 – the percentage varies slightly by state. The cosigner then guarantees to the bail agent that he will pay the full $25,000 if the defendant does not appear in court.

The cosigner is a friend or family member who signs all the paperwork required to have the defendant released from jail. The cosigner promises to ensure that the defendant will show up in court or will pay the full amount of the bond. The cosigner's guarantee usually comes in the form of collateral.

Collateral is something of value used to secure a loan, e.g., real estate, car, boat, etc. A bail bond is essentially a loan. If the defendant fails to appear in court, the loan must be repaid. The collateral must be something the bail agent can confiscate if the defendant fails to show and the loan is not repaid.

The bail agent does not pay the court the bail amount in cash, even if cash collateral is offered. The bail agent posts bail in the form of a promissory note known as a bail bond. The bond is the bail agent's promise to the court that if the defendant fails to appear, the bail amount will be paid in full. Because the bail agent is liable to the court for the full amount of bail, it's important that the collateral be valued at the full bail amount. Otherwise, the bail agent will be required to make up the difference.

In the example above, where the full amount of bail is $25,000, if the bail agent accepts as collateral a car worth $10,000 and the defendant skips town, the bail agent will have to repossess the car. Assuming he can sell the car for $10,000, which is not a given, he will be short $15,000 for the full amount.

If, on the other hand, the bond is secured by a homeowner, the bail agent is almost assured he will receive the full $25,000 if the defendant doesn't meet his obligations. The homeowner will not want to lose his home and will find a way to obtain the full amount, perhaps by refinancing the property.

The bail agent has many considerations when bailing a

defendant out of jail. One of the most important considerations: What is the defendant charged with? If the crime is not that serious, less risk may be involved. The bail agent then determines what type of collateral he requires for such a bond.

When a defendant is facing jail time on a more serious crime, collateral is a must. A person faced with drug trafficking, child endangerment, molestation and other serious charges are likely to fail to appear in court. Therefore, the bail agent needs a guarantee of sufficient collateral before taking on one of these cases. It is always better to be safe than sorry.

One crime that is not so serious but poses a high risk for the bail agent is prostitution. This charge carries a very low bail amount but is considered risky. As a general rule in the bail industry, prostitutes do not typically show up for court. Why not? Many of them have drug problems. They know that most courts will require them to do 90 days of jail time – typical for California. They would much rather skip town, go back to work and feed their addiction than spend 90 days in jail.

Do you have what it takes to become a bail agent?

Clearly a bail agent's success depends on solid risk assessment. But more than that is required to open a bail bond agency and build a thriving business. Do you have what it takes?

As with any business, it helps if you're entrepreneurial, self-motivated and aggressive. Strong marketing, management and interpersonal skills don't hurt either. The skills critical to running other businesses are the same skills required to build a successful bail bond agency. Remember, we're not talking about Hollywood stereotypes. As a bail agent, you will be a serious business professional and you need to run your business accordingly.

1. Marketing skills

Marketing requires the ability to assess the competition (*see Chapter 5 – Starting Your Own Bail Bond Business*). Your marketing strategy might start with the yellow pages, where most people turn when they're looking for a bail agent. Before placing an ad, you will need to review existing ads, compare ad sizes, cost and popularity of each type of yellow book.

To promote your bail bond business, you will also need to learn how to network with criminal defense attorneys, who are an important source of client referrals. To network effectively, you will need to distinguish your agency from the competition. Internet, word of mouth and business classified ads are a few other approaches to marketing with which you will need to become comfortable and competent.

2. Management skills

Strong management skills are essential to a successful bail bond business. A bail agent must be able to manage money, people, office files and phones – 24 hours a day, 7 days a week. Most bail agents never close their doors. They are always available. Calls often come at the most inconvenient times and the bail agent must be ready to jump when the phone rings. Expect many dinners, movies and parties and sleep to be interrupted.

To run your bail bond business well, you must have the discipline to keep track of all your defendants – by talking to them on a daily basis or following up with the court to be sure all of your clients have appeared. You'll learn that you need to have a change of clothes with you at all times. It happens often that an attorney will call you when you are at the gym, at the beach, playing with the kids at the park, and you will need to be in court within the hour. If you have a change of clothes, you will be prepared to change in your car. You need to be ready to go at a moment's notice.

3. Computer skills

You also need to have basic computer skills. You will need to have a management software program for your records. This can be a bail bond software program or a simple program like ACT or Microsoft Access. You will need to know how to look up real property addresses on your computer. You should also know how to use a word processing program and a spreadsheet program.

Bail agents work in a competitive environment. If your competitors are saving time and money by using special software or Internet search programs, you will need to do the same. Computers also facilitate letter writing and keeping track of correspondence.

As the criminal justice system becomes increasingly electronic, you will need to rely on your computer skills more and more. Many courts and jails are putting their records online now. Soon you will no longer need to call the courts for information. You will be able to access their records directly from your computer. If you need to obtain information on a potential client in custody, his information might be online for your convenience. This allows you almost immediate access to his file. Your clients will think you are tied into the law enforcement and court systems.

You will also find computer skills helpful when a defendant skips town. Several programs allow you to pay to access personal records and perform background checks. These programs can help you locate a defendant that has absconded.

4. Licensing and continuing education

To become a bail agent, you don't need a four-year college degree, but some training is required. Most states require that you be a U.S. citizen, a high school graduate, a resident of the state in which you are applying for a license and at least 18 years of age. In most states, you begin by taking a pre-licensing course – in California, for example, this is a two-day course offered by the Bail Bond Association for the State of California. Then you take the Department of Insurance (DOI) bail exam. When you pass the exam, you get your license. In most states, you also need to take a continuing education class every year (*see Chapter 5 – Starting Your Own Bail Bond Business*).

5. Start-up capital

You're starting a business, so you need some overhead money to purchase essentials: a business phone, cell phone, pager, a reliable car, computer, fax, photocopier, a small office space and some advertising.

Many bail bond agencies are started from a home office to keep overhead low. As your practice grows, you can get an office close to a jail or courthouse. Your overhead will increase, but so will your visibility. The exposure to new clients should more than pay for the cost of office space. Put a large sign on your door so potential clients know you are there.

Some bail agent businesses apply for corporation status for tax purposes, but that doesn't mean the agency is big and employs a large staff of agents. One person can create a corporation. An accountant can tell you the best form of business to establish.

The amount of start-up capital you need for a bail bond agency depends on your strategy. You can start your business for as little as $10,000. If you plan to go into the yellow pages and begin advertising immediately, you will need a little extra money to carry you through the first few months of advertising. This is where it gets tricky and where most new bail agents make mistakes.

Let's say you plan to spend $1,000 per month on advertising in the first three months, and you need another $2,000 a month to live on. The first few weeks are slow, with no calls coming in. Suddenly the phone rings and it's a prospective client with a $10,000 bail, which means a 10% premium, or $1,000 fee payable to you. At this point you are desperate to earn some money, because you have bills coming in. A $1,000 income from this client would be very nice.

It's critical to remember the risk factor here. Evaluate why you are writing this bond. Is it because you trust this client and he has the collateral, or is it because you want the

$1,000? If the bond is a good risk, that's fine. But if it's a questionable risk, and you only want to write the bond to cover part of your monthly expenses, you should not write it. If the defendant skips town, you will face a $10,000 loss.

This is one reason discipline and management skills are so important to a bail agent. Later in this chapter, and in Chapter 5, we will look more closely at these financial issues.

The BUF account

When you start your bail bond agency, you will need to open a Build Up Fund (BUF) account. What is a BUF account? When you become a bail agent, you need a surety company to back you. The surety company guarantees every bond you write. The BUF is a type of bond-guarantee account that the surety company holds for you.

You will be required to deposit 10% of your earnings into this account. At the end of your career, when all of your clients' cases are closed, the money in this account will be returned to you. Therefore, you should think of the BUF as a retirement account.

The BUF is designed to guarantee your surety company that you will not write "bad bail" and that if you do, you will have money in this account to pay for it. "Bad bail" means bailing a person out of jail just to earn your premium, without considering the client's risk factor.

The backing of a surety company is critical, and it's difficult to obtain this backing at first. A surety company will not support you unless you have a license and some experience in the industry. One way to obtain this experience is to start by working for an existing bail agency.

Most bail agents are sole proprietors, however. They run their own business and are their own primary employee. This is a competitive industry, so partnerships are rare. Therefore, a General Agent (GA) might be necessary when you first enter the bail bond industry.

A GA is a bail agent that acts as a middleman between the surety company and you. Where the surety company won't take a risk on you, because you have no experience, the GA might. The GA will allow you to be self-employed but will keep a close watch on you to ensure you are writing good bail. The GA will help train you and give you advice for every type of situation (*see Chapter 3 – Meet the Key Players*).

A typical day for a bail agent

Remember that being a bail agent is not a nine-to-five job. People are arrested 24 hours a day, seven days a week, 365 days a year. People are arrested on Christmas and during the Super Bowl – perhaps especially during the Super Bowl. When you're not bailing someone out of jail, you might be participating in bail associations at the county, state and national levels or attending seminars, which will take up more of your time. And don't forget that you have to meet your state's continuing education requirements. As a successful bail agent, you will have more than a full time job, but your time will be rewarded.

What might a typical day be like in your new career? You can expect to be surrounded by law enforcement professionals from probation, police and sheriff's departments. You might need to meet with jailers, watch commanders, court clerks, attorneys and occasionally judges. Obtaining court information will take a large part of your day.

On any given day, you might post bail for one client, return collateral to another client who fulfilled his obligations, or follow up on a client who skipped town and forfeited the bail bond you so carefully posted. You might check with the court for exonerations on past clients. You might need to call people who owe you money so you can collect from them. You might focus on marketing and office clutter clearing.

The number of cases you handle in a given day can vary. You might go three days without needing to bail someone out of jail, and then on the fourth day you might bail out seven people. It all depends on how often the phone rings, who needs your services and when.

At the end of the day, you might find yourself with a nice income for a day's work. The bail bond business offers a lucrative return on time invested. However, as a self-employed businessperson, you must stay on top of your finances. Even if you hire an accountant to manage your money, you will need to know a little about bookkeeping. Most of all, you will need discipline to manage your business and finances well.

More about fees and finances

An aggressive bail agent can earn anywhere from $100,000 to $1 million in a matter of two to three years. When a bail agent makes money, it is usually in large sums – $500, $1000, $2,500 or more at a time. The money earned is known as a premium, which is the fee that a bail agent charges each client for posting a bail bond.

The bail agent's fee is a specific percentage of the total bail amount. Most states have a 10% rule. This means your clients will pay you a fee of 10% on every bond you write. Some states are on a sliding scale. Other states allow fees of 15% (*see Chapter 4 – How Bail Works*).

When a person is charged with a crime, a bail amount is associated with that crime. When a client calls to post bail for someone who was arrested, you will need to meet with that client, collect your fee, and have the client sign all the necessary paperwork and deposit whatever collateral was agreed upon. If the client offers cash collateral, you must hold that money in a fiduciary capacity. To do so, you are required to have a trust account open at all times. The cash collateral goes into the trust account while the premium goes into your business account.

Sometimes it is very enticing to spend the premium right away – perhaps as a down payment toward that new car you've been eyeing. Rather than spend the money right away, you should anticipate times when your business might not be booming. You need to save some money to carry the business through slow times. Your business might slow for a few days or a week or even a month.

Likewise, it's not wise to make too many lifestyle changes as your income increases. Give it a few years to truly establish a good, solid, long-lasting business. Most often, if your spending habits are under control and you are disciplined with the money you earn, your business will survive the slow times and will become successful over time.

While the importance of saving money to keep your business running might seem like common sense, it's unfortunate that many new bail agents don't follow this advice. Many new agents last only a few years in the business, because they tire of the long hours and lack the discipline to save money. They want to earn as much as possible as quickly as possible, and then they run into problems. As with all businesses, success as a bail agent comes with consistent good practices, diligence and discipline.

Earlier in this chapter, we talked about the danger of trying to build your business too quickly and taking on clients just for the fees you can earn. Let's look at this danger in more detail.

When you first start out as a bail agent, you might be tempted to post bonds for as many clients as possible, in order to collect your premiums and build your business quickly. Everyone who calls your office represents potential income, so you are eager to post bail for each one. This is when your consideration of flight risk is critical. If the defendant skips town, you will be worse off financially than if you declined the job. If you take on a client just for the immediate income from your premium, without pre-screening and interviewing the client carefully, you could be headed for serious trouble.

Many clients are able to pay the premium but don't have collateral or cannot be trusted while out on bail. Bailing out one bad-risk client without collateral can have a lasting effect on your business.

Let's say you become desperate or greedy and post a $25,000 bond without collateral. You earn a $2,500 premium. With that, you can pay all your bills, go out for a nice dinner and consider getting a new car. Business is rolling and everything looks great.

What happens when you receive a notice from the court three months later, indicating that the defendant did not show up for court and you now have a limited time to locate him? Suddenly that $2,500 you earned doesn't look so great, and you wish you could turn back the clock and turn down that client.

There is nothing like opening a court notice indicating that your client failed to appear, and then remembering that you don't even have collateral from that client. What are you going to do now? If the defendant skips town and the cosigner has no collateral, your only option is to sue them for the full amount of the bail. This is a really bad situation. Now you are using your savings to hire an attorney to sue someone from whom you probably won't recover any money.

What if the cosigner takes off as well? I've been in situations where the defendant and the cosigner skipped town and ended up in another country. The bottom line is that you have to be ready for anything. If you don't have collateral from the client and you are not 100% positive the defendant will show up for court, be careful! It's better to turn away a potential client than to be on the wrong end of a forfeited bond.

It is said that it takes approximately 18 bonds of equal size to pay off one forfeiture. This means that if a client skips town on a $10,000 bond, for which you earned merely a $1,000 premium, you will need to write 18 additional $10,000 bonds just to pay for that one forfeiture. Why so many? The 18 bonds will earn you a total of $18,000 in premiums. Subtract from that total your salary, advertising costs, BUF, office rent, employees, any additional expenses… and you just might have enough left over to pay the $10,000 forfeiture.

This isn't meant to scare you away from becoming a bail agent. If you're willing to work hard and manage your money wisely, the bail bond industry could be the right career for you.

The following chapters will expand on the concepts introduced in this chapter, to give you a more thorough look at the bail bond industry. You will learn how to write bail the right way. You will learn what to look for when you pre-screen and interview clients. You will learn how to market your business, manage your employees, run a successful business and ultimately enjoy your new career. For the right person, a bail bond business can be a very rewarding enterprise.

2

THE HISTORY OF BAIL

This chapter was written by Gerald P. Monks, Esq. Reprinted with permission.

When the United States was formed, the first American law enforcement officers discovered that corn was not the only thing growing in the New World: crime was sprouting up as well. Instead of inventing a new system of bail provisions and court procedures, it was easier for them to rely on English statutes that had been tested for hundreds of years. The American system has evolved over time; however, knowing the history of the English system will help you understand American bail structure.

For as long as human beings have gotten into trouble, they've worked to find ways to get out of it. Back in medieval England, officers of the court discovered a major flaw in human nature: people accused of crimes preferred not to show up to face possible punishment. You can hardly blame them: medieval punishment included water torture and burning at the stake.

And yet local sheriffs couldn't keep everyone locked up until trial because there wasn't a magistrate in every town, so it might be months before a judge was available to hear a case in a certain area. This meant that after a month or so, there just wasn't room to house all those poachers and vandals and traitors in the small town jail. So officials eager to witness a good water torture developed methods to insure that the accused citizens would appear for trial once they were released from the crowded jails.

The responsibility for deciding who would be released from jail fell to local sheriffs, who were given a good deal of authority by the king. The sheriffs had several options. One was to release the suspect to a person who offered "personal surety," meaning that the other person would bear the punishment in the suspect's place if the suspect didn't show up in court. This loyal friend would much rather see his friend burn at the stake than to go up in flames himself.

But there were no rules, so the sheriff could release or hold suspects using any standard, weighing factors like the severity of the crime, whether the suspect was a flight risk, and whether the suspect was the sheriff's best friend or could offer a bribe. Thus, this broad authority brought out another flaw in human nature: the tendency to exploit the system for personal gain.

In 1275, Parliament passed the Statute of Westminster to remove some of the temptation from sheriffs. The statute specifically listed which crimes were bailable offenses and which were not. After that, bail law remained largely unchanged for several hundred years, an amazing fact considering the number of problems that remained in the system.

In the early seventeenth century, King Charles I was short

on cash. He didn't get any money from Parliament, which at the time could withhold payment from the king whenever it felt like it. And this Parliament didn't care much for Charles. When he wasn't ruling the kingdom, he loved spending money, especially on expensive artwork by Raphael and Titian. To support his art habit, he hit up some of his noblemen for loans. "I'll pay you back after I crush Scotland," he probably said. He didn't take no for an answer. Those who refused to lend him money were imprisoned without bail. The king wouldn't even inform the prisoners of the charges against them, for good reason: the charges were illegal. Knights had no obligation to lend the king their hard-earned money. They had rescued a lot of damsels in distress to get that money.

Five of these incarcerated knights, upon discovering that lawyers had already been invented, filed a habeas corpus petition. (*Habeas corpus* is a Latin phrase that evolved into a legal term. It means someone in jail wants to be brought before the court to complain because he thinks he is being unlawfully detained.) The knights' petition argued that they could not be held indefinitely without trial or bail.

When the case was brought before the court, the lawyers for the knights argued that since the five were being denied a trial, they were being kept in jail solely on the basis of an accusation. Because no attorney or court official was being allowed to examine the evidence, that accusation could very well be unsubstantiated, they said. Because the knights weren't even told their offenses, they were being denied the right to petition for bail. The king had, in effect, found them guilty and sentenced them to jail all on his own.

The attorney general – yes, they already had an attorney general back then. They had everything in their legal system except Court TV – contended that the king had the sovereign power to imprison citizens as he saw fit and was perfectly capable of balancing their right to freedom against the interests of national security. The court showed its trust in the king's judgment by upholding this argument, obviously forgetting the flaws in human nature that had already been uncovered by the country's fledgling judicial system.

Parliament responded to the court's ruling with the Petition of Right of 1628. England already had the Magna Carta, which said that "No Freeman shall be taken or imprisoned… but by lawful judgment of his Peers, or by the Law of the Land." But apparently that law was hard to enforce after 400 years. The Petition of 1628 noted that the king had imprisoned people "without any cause showed" and concluded that no one could be detained without being informed of the specific accusation against him.

By requiring that a person be informed of the cause for arrest, the Petition of Right of 1628 provided a suspect with valuable knowledge. Now a suspect could turn to the Statute of Westminster to see which list his crime appeared on: bailable or unbailable.

But once again the dark side of human nature rose to the challenge. Court officials found a way around the Petition of Right through a new legal tactic: stalling. This tactic was most evident in the case of Francis Jenkes. In 1676, Jenkes gave a speech asking for a new Parliament to be called to fix some problems in the kingdom. He was charged with sedition and jailed. Sedition was a nasty charge akin to treason; it basically prohibited citizens from saying bad things about the king.

Jenkes felt the charge was a little vague and sought a writ of habeas corpus. He was denied, first because the court was taking a vacation and later because the case was not scheduled on the court calendar. Jenkes was no legal eagle, but he thought the obvious solution would be to put the case on the court calendar. He asked the court to schedule the case so that his writ could be heard. The court stubbornly refused. Jenkes remained in jail for months.

In response to cases like Jenkes' where procedural delays were used to deny the suspect's rights, Parliament passed the Habeas Corpus Act of 1677. The act specified that a magistrate had to release a prisoner unless his offense was unbailable. It eliminated the ability of courts to rely on procedural delays to keep a prisoner detained.

Although the Habeas Corpus Act improved the rights of suspects, it had a loophole, and it didn't take long for unscrupulous sheriffs to find it. The act didn't specify how much bail could be imposed. Therefore, even suspects accused of bailable offenses would be stuck in jail if the sheriff decided to set excessive bail. A poor farmer who got on the sheriff's bad side might not have a stack of gold coins to meet the bail requirements and would have to languish in jail until his trial, even if his crime was minor. Since the king had a close relationship with the sheriffs, the king's enemies could always expect excessive bail.

By now Parliament was really ticked off at having its attempts to provide justice thwarted at every turn. When it learned of this latest scam, it responded with the English Bill of Rights of 1689, which accused the king of attempting "to subvert...the laws and liberties of the kingdom" by requiring excessive bail. The Bill of Rights declared simply, "Excessive bail ought not to be required."

In early America, colonists followed English laws until the colonies became independent in 1776. Then they enacted their own laws about bail and other such legal issues. Most laws drew from the British system: Section 9 of Virginia's Constitution in 1776 had a familiar ring to it when it declared simply that "excessive bail ought not to be required." In 1785, this provision was strengthened by a statute that gave judges rules for applying bail, specifying that those accused of manslaughter or other crimes "punishable by life or limb" should not be granted bail.

The Virginia constitution laid the groundwork for the new country's Bill of Rights. The Eighth Amendment of the U.S. Constitution was taken virtually verbatim from Section 9 of the Virginia Constitution: "Excessive bail shall not be required, nor excessive fines imposed, nor cruel and unusual punishment inflicted." Similarly, the Sixth Amendment echoes the English Habeas Corpus Act of 1678 by insuring that a person who is arrested "be informed of the nature and cause of the accusation" so he can demand bail if he has committed a bailable offense.

These basic concepts had already been tested for hundred of years and would stand a few hundred more. In 1789, Congress passed the Judiciary Act, which would frame the fundamental bail statute that remained in force until 1966. The act specified which types of crime were bailable. Generally the capital offenses – murder, treason, espionage, and other crimes punishable by the death penalty or life imprisonment – were not as bailable as noncapital offenses. The act also set bounds on judges' discretion in setting bail.

After almost 200 years, Congress finally updated America's bail laws with the Bail Reform Act of 1966. It stated that a defendant facing trial for a noncapital offense should be released "on his personal recognizance" or on personal bond. However, if an officer of the court had reason to suspect the defendant would skip town, the judge could choose a more restrictive alternative: limiting the defendant's travel, executing an appearance bond that was refunded when the defendant appeared in court, etc. Basically, the act said that most offenders should be set free with as few obstacles as possible unless they had been arrested for a crime for which they faced the death penalty. If the defendant had ties to the community, he or she would be set free regardless of other circumstances.

Keep in mind that these were federal guidelines. Most states had their own rules, but many added guidelines similar to the Bail Reform Act after 1966.

The District of Columbia was the first to point out the flaws in the act. Residents of The District, which isn't actually a state, had to follow the federal law, and they didn't like the idea that a defendant's potential danger to the community wasn't considered in the bail process for noncapital offenses, especially considering the number of crimes being committed by defendants out on bail. So a revision was made – The District of Columbia Court Reform and Criminal Procedure Act of 1970 allowed judges to consider dangerousness to the community as well as risk of flight when setting bail in noncapital cases.

The rest of the federal system got on board with the Bail Reform Act of 1984, which added the safety of the community as a factor that could be considered when imposing bail. Under the new guidelines, a person can be detained without bail if he:

1. Poses a risk to the community.
2. May intimidate jurors or witnesses or otherwise obstruct justice while out on bail.
3. Committed a violent or drug offense, an offense carrying a penalty of death or of life in prison, or committed any felony while already having a serious criminal record.

Those are the basic concepts behind the modern bail system. The specific bail policies and amounts may vary from court to court, but the underlying principle is the same: citizens accused of certain crimes and meeting certain criteria are entitled to be released from jail as they wait for their day in court.

REFERENCES

DeVol, Laura. "The Evolution of Bail."
http://www.gwu.edu/~pretrial/page13.htm
"Charles I." Kings and Queens of the United Kingdom.
http://www.royal.gov.uk
"Charles I (1625-49AD)."
http://www.Brittania.com/history/monarchs/mon47.html
Freedman, Eric. "Milestones in Habeas Corpus, Part I."
http://www.law.ua.edu/lawreview/freedman512.htm

3

MEET THE KEY PLAYERS

Although most bail agents are sole proprietors who work alone, they aren't isolated. The success of their business depends on a network of companies, agencies and individuals that keep the bail system running. Understanding who these key players are and what they contribute is important to establishing a successful bail bond agency.

Surety companies

A surety company is an insurance company. It provides financial support and backing to the bail agent and certifies to the courts that funds are available to pay the full bail amount if the defendant doesn't show.

The courts view the surety company as the ultimate source of payment, because the surety company issues the actual bail bond. Like the bail agency, the surety company is a business and needs to earn a profit. That won't happen if the surety company is constantly paying on forfeited bail bonds, particularly without receiving anything in return. Therefore, before it will write a bond or guarantee payment on behalf of a client, the surety company wants indemnity.

Indemnity is a term used often in the insurance industry. It means security or protection against loss. As such, the cosigner of the bond is sometimes called the indemnitor. Before agreeing to back a bail agent, the surety company might request indemnity in the form of collateral plus a written guarantee from the bail agent that he will follow good practices. The surety company wants to ensure that the bail agent is not likely to end up with many forfeitures.

The relationship between surety company and bail agent begins when the bail agent contacts a surety company and requests a meeting with the bail department. He completes an application and signs an agreement stating that he is financially liable for every bond he writes. The surety company will expect that the applicant has passed the appropriate licensing exam for his state and has gained experience working as a bail agent.

The surety company will run a credit and background check on the bail agent and require him to set up a BUF account. The BUF will be used as collateral in the event the bail agent defaults on a bond. If the bail agent can't provide the cash to open a BUF account, the surety company may ask for a lien on real estate the bail agent owns.

Once the bail agent meets all the surety company's requirements, the company files a request with the DOI to have the applicant appointed as a bail agent for that company. The surety company fills out the necessary forms and provides a photo identification of the agent to the DOI.

What benefit does a surety company derive from its relationship with the bail agent? The surety company receives a bond fee – a percentage of the fee paid to a bail agent for each bond written. The surety company knows that successful bail agents will look for opportunities to write bail bonds and other types of bonds offered, which means greater income for the surety company.

The bail agent benefits from the relationship too. Along with providing the much-needed financial backing, surety companies can provide bail agents with other useful services, such as helping bail agents with skip tracing, collections, lawsuits and other legal matters. Because the surety company's financial interests are at stake, often the company will keep track of cases and notify the bail agent when his cases are closed. Each surety company offers its own range of services and has its own advantages and disadvantages.

A bail agent can be appointed to more than one surety company, provided he meets the requirements of each. Why would an agent want to be backed by more than one surety company? Different companies offer different financial products, and a bail agent might want more variety to choose from. For example, some surety companies issue only bail bonds while others also write different types of bonds, such as immigration and civil bonds (*see Chapter 8 – Other Types of Bonds*).

Another factor bail agents weigh when choosing a surety company is its writing authority. All surety companies have a state-approved writing authority, which sets the maximum amount per bond the surety company can write in that state. This amount is based on a rating system from the DOI. The rating system operates similar to consumer credit scores.

While it's not necessary for the bail agent to understand

all the calculations involved in the DOI's rating, it is important to know the maximum amount of a bond the agent can write under a particular surety. Based on a bail agent's creditworthiness, a surety company may set a limit on the dollar amount of bonds the agent can issue. The surety company will require that the agent call for approval on any bond over that limit.

Once a bail agent is appointed to a surety company, he is given an account number. A bail agent's account may be cancelled for several reasons:

1. Exceeding the writing authority.
2. Producing excessive forfeitures.
3. Breaking the law.

Cancellation of an agent's account can end his career in the bail bond business permanently.

Communication between the bail agent and the surety company takes several forms, depending on the purpose of the communication. A bail agent will simply call the surety company to ask a question, to obtain approval for writing a bond that exceeds his writing authority, or to post a transfer bond for an out-of-town client (*see Chapter 6 – Running a Bail Bond Business*).

When submitting a bond, however, communication between the bail agent and surety company is always in writing. The surety provides bail agents with envelopes in which written bonds are sent via registered mail along with two separate checks, one for the surety company's percentage (bond cost) and the other for the agent's reserve account or

BUF. In addition, if the bail amount is high, the surety company will want the agent to submit proof of the property provided as collateral, so that the company has the appropriate information if the defendant does not appear in court and the company needs to foreclose on the property.

A bail agent can obtain more blank bonds only after he has submitted the bonds he's already written to the surety company, along with the appropriate payments. The bail agent will not be issued more bonds until he has paid his bond cost on the bonds he has written. Most of the time, bail agents will have a sufficient supply of bonds to last for a month. Sometimes the surety company will give bail agents a certain number of individual bond powers, e.g., two $100,000's, five $50,000's, ten $25,000's and fifteen $10,000's (*see Chapter 5 – Starting Your Own Bail Bond Business*).

Bail agents should file a report to their surety company every week, whether they write one bond or 25 bonds. If they wait longer, the report is larger and the money owed is greater. For example, if an agent has written 25 bonds over a month without reporting to the surety company, the agent might owe thousands of dollars, which can become discouraging. But paying five or six bonds every week is a manageable amount of money and paperwork. Regular reporting also keeps the agent on track as to how many bonds he has left.

One reason it's important to keep track: Once you are out of $100,000 power bonds, you will not be able to write another $100,000 bond if you haven't paid your bond cost and BUF fees for the $100,000 powers you were issued. Even if you have two $50,000 powers, you cannot put them together to make a $100,000 bond. Reporting weekly – regardless of how many bonds you write – will keep you fully stocked with bonds, so you don't lose a client because you lack sufficient bonds. Keeping a full stock is important, because when it rains in this business, it pours.

General agents

Because so much is at stake in backing a bail bond, it isn't easy for a new bail agent to obtain the support of a surety company. Until a bail agent acquires the experience necessary to establish a relationship with a surety company, he might need to depend on the support of a general agent (GA).

A GA is a licensed bail agent who is well established in the business and has a strong relationship with his surety company. The surety company qualifies him as a GA, allowing him to sell bonds to other bail agents. The GA acts as an intermediary for the new agent. The GA screens the new bail agent to be sure he is trustworthy and can handle the responsibility. Through this arrangement, GAs can expand their operations, thereby generating more revenue for themselves and the surety company.

A bail agent who works directly with a surety company is required to pay a percentage of his premium to the surety company, as a bond cost. When a new bail agent works with a GA, the GA will add a percentage to the bond cost. For example, on a $10,000 bond, typically the bail agent will receive a fee of 10%, or $1,000 from the client. The bond cost to the surety company would be 10% of that fee, or $100. The GA might charge the bail agent 15%, which in this case would be $150. The GA then pays the surety company the

$100 bond cost and keeps the difference – $50 in this case – as profit.

GAs don't work only with new agents. Sometimes an established bail agent will work with a GA. This arrangement allows an experienced bail agent to have access to higher underwriting authority without needing to go through the approval process required by the surety company.

For example, let's say a bail agent has only $25,000 in underwriting authority. He receives a call from a client who needs a bond for $100,000. He calls his GA who has the authority to write a bond for $100,000. A bond in that amount would earn the bail agent a premium of $10,000. Of that amount, the primary bail agent collects his usual fee of 10% on the $25,000 he was authorized to write, or $2,500. Then he and the GA split the remaining $7,500 balance of the premium, or $3,750 each. The primary bail agent pays the bond cost to the surety company on the $25,000 portion of the bond. The bond cost on the remaining $75,000 is typically split between the bail agent and the GA.

The terms of the arrangements are negotiated and placed in writing before a permanent relationship is established between bail agents and GAs. The written agreement should be detailed and address a variety of circumstances to minimize potential conflicts.

Liability is also split. This means the bail agent is liable for the amount specified in the terms of the split. For example, if the agreement between the two agents calls for a 50/50 split, the GA would be liable in this case for $37,500, which is half of the $75,000 bond being split. The primary bail agent would be liable for his original $25,000 plus an additional $37,500 (the other half of the $75,000 bond) for a total of $62,500.

In summary, the GA provides a training ground for new bail agents and is a source of opportunity and income for established bail agents. The bail agent should remember that the GA is also sometimes a direct competitor. A GA might even advertise in the same yellow pages you do and have ads in the same areas where you have yours.

Law enforcement

Without law enforcement agencies, the entire criminal justice system would be out of work. Bail agents are not technically involved in law enforcement, but they frequently deal with police, sheriffs and marshals at jails or court facilities.

The law enforcement officer that a bail agent comes into contact with most frequently is the jailer. In smaller jails, a bail agent meets directly with the jailer. In large county jails, the bail agent will drop off the bond at the front desk for processing, never meeting the jailer. Jails and jailers are always busy. Their job is tedious and requires that they be meticulous. Therefore, you should be patient and respectful of their time.

The primary role of law enforcement officers is "to serve and protect" the public, not to assist bail agents. Interaction between law enforcement officers and bail agents is minimal. But law enforcement officers play a critical role in the bail process.

A police officer, sheriff or marshal will arrest a citizen suspected of or engaging in criminal activity. The arresting officer creates the arrest report that a bail agent relies on for information, including the appropriate bail amount from the bail schedule.

Law enforcements officers have a difficult job. It's important that the bail agent not make their job harder. Tension might arise. Officers might become frustrated when they see that the perpetrator they worked so hard to put away is being let out of jail. Keep your perspective. Remember that they work with difficult people day in and day out. Don't be confrontational. Be patient and respectful. Always be polite to them.

Bail associations

Bail associations are nonprofit organizations run by bail agents to improve the industry, promote a positive image and lobby for legislation on behalf of bail agents. Membership in a bail association is voluntary but highly recommended.

Unlike the bar association for attorneys, the bail association has no control over a bail agent's training or testing, though the associations participate in the process. The DOI publishes, administers and grades the exams, but often the state's bail association offers pre-licensing courses and supplies candidates with the materials to pass the bail test.

The industry's national association, Professional Bail Agents of the United States (http://www.pbus.com), founded in 1981, promotes the professional growth of bail agents. It hosts two annual conventions and works to provide networking opportunities and improve educational standards. It also lobbies on behalf of bail agents in support of legislation related to the bail bond industry. It has over 14,000 members nationwide.

Although most associations are organized at the state level, some agents form local or county associations that help in establishing relationships with local law enforcement agencies and judges. Improved relationships help create better communication channels. If a problem arises with bail agents illegally distributing business cards on government property, for example, the law enforcement liaison to the bail association can pass the concerns along, so that the bail association can warn its members and educate them on proper marketing techniques. Or if a jail needs to establish a more efficient policy for processing defendants being released on bail and thereby alleviate overcrowding, the bail association can provide input and then inform its members of any new procedures implemented at the jail.

Programs sponsored by bail associations can improve a bail agent's knowledge and efficiency. For example, bail associations frequently invite high-level members of local law enforcement agencies or court representatives to speak at meetings. This allows bail agents to have their questions addressed and to learn more about the inner workings of the criminal justice system. In summary, bail agent associations are critical to maintaining a unity between licensed agents and other key players in the bail industry.

Bail enforcement agents

Another key figure in a bail agent's professional life is the bail enforcement agent (BEA). The BEA only comes into play when things go wrong. BEAs, commonly known as bounty hunters, are investigators that specialize in locating skips. They are trained in arrest techniques and procedures. They will typically go anywhere to catch anyone at anytime. BEAs have been known to search for skips from their local area to foreign countries like Germany, Vietnam and South America. We will discuss the role of the BEA in Chapter 7.

4

HOW BAIL WORKS: THE SIMPLE VERSION

Setting bail

Let's walk through a simple bail bond process. A woman named Nora decides to go on a shopping spree and writes bad checks to pay for everything. She's caught, arrested and taken to jail. The bail process begins immediately.

In the United States, Nora is presumed innocent until proven guilty. She isn't charged with a capital offense and she poses no danger to the community. Therefore, she is entitled to bail under the Bail Reform Acts of 1966 and 1984.

If Nora were arrested for murder, she would be detained in jail until she could appear before a judge, who would decide whether she should be released on bail and, if so, for how much. For a murder case, when bail is granted the amount is steep, often set at $1 million or more.

Even when a murder hasn't been committed, the arresting officer has the right to treat a case as a "no-bail" case, meaning the defendant is required to see a judge before bail is set. This typically occurs with serious crimes or when the defendant is arrested on a no-bail warrant. Defendants charged with rape or serious drug-related crimes are usually held without bail until the judge can see them, and even then, the judge might deny them bail.

Nora has not committed murder or a no-bail crime. She has written bad checks to buy a new wardrobe at several different stores. This is a typical bail situation. Most arrests in the United States are for non-capital offenses (crimes in which murder or treason is not committed) like Nora's.

The arresting officer creates an arrest report for Nora. Consulting the penal code for his area, he looks up the charge for writing bad checks. He writes down the statute in the penal code that Nora is alleged to have violated, as well as the corresponding bail amount from the bail schedule. In the county where Nora is arrested, the crime of writing bad checks calls for $20,000 in bail.

The amount of bail depends on the severity of the charge. While a murder charge can carry a bail amount in excess of $1 million, a minor violation such as an outstanding traffic ticket might call for only $1,000 in bail. Even within a particular category of charges, the amount of bail varies. For example, a drug charge can vary from "possession for personal use" to "possession for sale." Someone possessing a small amount of narcotics might face $10,000 in bail. Someone with a trunk full of narcotics is probably looking to sell and might have bail set at $100,000 or more.

Who creates the bail schedule? Local judges convene to set appropriate bail amounts for specific crimes, and they update the schedule regularly. In California, these amounts are usually determined on a county-by-county basis and become part of the California Penal Code. For drug-related crimes, the bail schedule is part of the California Health and Safety Code. For traffic tickets, the bail schedule is part of the Vehicle Code.

After the arresting officer in Nora's case determines her bail amount from the bail schedule, she and her arrest record are turned over to the jailer. If this is her first arrest and the damages she caused are minor, she might be interviewed by a detention release officer and released on her own recognizance, which means she simply promises to appear in court when she is required. In the business, this is referred to as "O.R." (own recognizance), "P.R." (personal recognizance) or "R.O.R." (released on own recognizance).

This form of bail is called public bail, which means the officials making the decisions about bail work for the government. Approximately one-fourth of arrestees in the United States are released on public bail.

In comparison to commercial bail that involves a bail agent, public bail has disadvantages. The officers making the decisions to release defendants face no consequences for their decisions. If their defendants don't show up for trial, the officers aren't required to pay the bond and they aren't assessed a penalty. In commercial bail, the bail agents weigh each decision carefully because they risk losing time and money, and they face the possibility of having to pay the full bail amount if the defendant fails to appear in court.

In public bail situations, if a defendant doesn't show up in court, the taxpayer bears the financial burden for locating the defendant. In commercial bail situations, the bail agent and cosigner pay these costs.

The system is tougher on defendants with a criminal record. If Nora did not have a criminal record or an active criminal case pending, she would have a 70% chance of being released on some type of bail, public or otherwise. If Nora were on parole or probation at the time of her arrest, however, she would have a less than 50% chance of being released – on any type of bail.

Let's say Nora has a history of defrauding people of their money. We know right away she will be denied the easy option of public bail. So her bail is set based on the bail schedule in that county: $20,000. Additional bail might be imposed if a background check reveals an outstanding warrant for another crime or additional information that changes the facts of the case.

The jailer tells Nora the bail amount. At this point, Nora will call a family member of friend to post bail for her, or she will call a bail agent directly. Many jails have lists of local bail agents on hand. If she calls a family member of friend, the jailer will explain the bail amount to them as well.

If Nora or her family member or friend has $20,000 in cash or in the bank, they can take that cash or a money order or cashier's check directly to the jail and post bail. They would not need the assistance of a bail agent. In Nora's case, she and her husband check their bank account balances and cannot come up with the full amount of the bail.

This situation is typical and it's not coincidental. The purpose of bail is to create a significant deterrent to stop Nora from fleeing the state and an incentive to ensure she makes her designated court appearance. Therefore, the bail amount is generally higher than most defendants have readily available. The defendant needs the help of other people – family member, friend, bail agent – who will also have a stake in ensuring the defendant does not skip town before trial.

Because she and her husband do not have the money to post bail, Nora hires a bail agent. The bail agent will decide whether or not to write a bail bond to release Nora from jail. Nora's decision to hire a bail agent is common. Approximately 37% of defendants released from custody are released on the commercial surety bonds written by a bail agent.

When the bail agent receives the call from Nora or her husband, he asks which jail she's in, what she is charged with and how much bail is required. He then provides a quote for his services – his premium, or fee – usually 10% of the total bail amount. He explains the collateral he will require to secure the bond.

The bail agent then calls the jail to obtain more detailed information, such as the date of Nora's first court appearance and her case number(s). He confirms the charges and her bail amount. The bail agent requires all of this information to complete the bail bond paperwork. After he has the information he needs, the bail agent begins the process of risk assessment.

Risk assessment

Assessing the risk in a bail case requires two major steps: 1) weighing the possibility that the individual being released will leave town to avoid prosecution and 2) determining whether the assets provided as collateral are worth enough to pay for the bond if the defendant skips. There is no chart to consult for risk assessment; no set of rules. It's based in part on the bail agent's experience and instincts and also on the defendant's past record and the stability of the defendant's current lifestyle.

The bail agent examines Nora's current lifestyle by asking a list of basic questions that will help him make the judgment call:

1. Does Nora live in the area?
2. Do most of her family members live in the area?
3. Is she employed? If so, how long has she worked for the same company or in the same industry?
4. Does she live in a house or apartment and for how long?
5. What are her personal assets?
6. Does she have any past criminal record?
7. What is the situation? What is the story behind the arrest?

These questions need to be answered not only by the defendant, but by the cosigner as well.

For cases where the bail amount is small and the crime is minor, a bail agent will typically know if he wants to write a bond after the first few minutes of speaking with a caller. For example, if parents call about their son who goes to school at Berkeley and was arrested for being drunk in public, the bail agent can tell pretty quickly that it's a good bond with a low risk. The student is facing very little punishment and is unlikely to leave his parents – who can provide the cash even if he does flee.

If the defendant's history is solid and the bond amount isn't large, the bail agent might not even require collateral to secure the bond. For instance, if the defendant is being bailed out by his parents, who have lived in the community for 30 years, and the defendant has served as executive of a local company for 10 years, the bail agent might decide that this is an easy case and write the bond without collateral. In an easy case like this, the bail agent might be ready to meet with the cosigner and sign the paperwork within 10 to 15 minutes of receiving the initial call.

Even in an easy case, however, risk is involved. Bail bonds always entail some degree of risk, and that risk always increases when a bail agent does not require collateral. You always have to consider the worst-case scenario. What if the defendant skips town? How will you recover the money you are now obligated to pay to the court? It is often a good idea to ask the cosigner up front: "How will you pay the bail amount if the defendant skips town?"

Some cases come with obvious red flags. For example, someone contacts you about his friend sitting in jail on a drug charge. The caller says he can pay your fee but he's skeptical about cosigning the bail bond. He adds that he's only known his friend for two years. This conversation should send a clear warning to you. The caller knows his friend better than you do. If he is reluctant to cosign, why would you want to write this bond?

When a defendant owns property, a cosigner might not be needed. However, the value of the collateral might become an issue. If the defendant has owned his property for only one year and has $30,000 equity in it, and his bail amount is $100,000, you have three options:

1. You can turn down the case.
2. You can accept the defendant's property as collateral.
3. You can ask for a cosigner.

Before you make your decision, you need to consider what will happen if the defendant doesn't appear in court and can't be located. If you write this $100,000 bond, secured only with collateral that has $30,000 equity, you will have very little to fall back on if the defendant skips town.

Every case is different, but assessing a defendant's ties to the community is always critical. If the defendant has been at his job for 10 years, has rented the same apartment for the last seven years and has lived in the area his entire life, then he might be an acceptable risk, especially if he is not facing serious charges.

For cases involving more serious crimes and higher bail amounts, the bail agent's risk is greater and therefore his risk assessment will take longer and be more thorough. Instinct plays an important role. If a bail agent is talking to the defendant or cosigner and suspects he is lying about the defendant's criminal record, the agent might want to do a thorough background check before agreeing to post bond.

A background check is also needed when the defendant might be a serious repeat offender and could face extended jail or prison time if convicted on his current charges. For example, California has a "three strikes" law. Criminals facing their third felony conviction face 25 years in prison.

These defendants are considered high risk.

It's always a good idea for the bail agent to know his clients inside and out. If he needs more information, he can hire a private investigator or use the services of companies that specialize in background checks. Many such companies exist, including Merlin Information Services (http://www.merlindata.com) and PeopleFind.com. Although public record searches usually require a small fee, they might save the bail agent money in the long run. You can never be too cautious when risking high amounts of money in the bail bond business.

Risk assessment is made easier if the court requires the defendant to wear a monitoring ankle bracelet. An ankle bracelet is occasionally used when the court believes the accused is a flight risk. When a bracelet is required, the defendant usually has only one day to report to a specified location to be fitted with the bracelet.

The ankle bracelet comes with a base-monitoring unit kept in the defendant's house. If the defendant strays too far from the base unit, the security company that provides the bracelet is alerted. The company will call the defendant's home two or three times. If the defendant doesn't answer, the company calls the police. The defendant has probably not gone far and can be found easily.

Ankle bracelets and similar monitoring devices are for the benefit of law enforcement officers as well as the bail agent. The bail agent isn't always informed right away when a defendant has left town. Regardless, any type of monitoring system that hinders the defendant's ability to leave town reduces the risk that the defendant will miss his court date.

Let's consider the bail agent's risk assessment of Nora. He decides she is not a flight risk. She is a lifetime resident of the community. All her family and friends are here. She has worked at the same restaurant for five years. She has one previous conviction, made all her court appearances and received a light sentence, which she served. The current charges against her are serious enough to require $20,000 in bail, but they are not so severe that she might run to Mexico to avoid prosecution.

Next, the bail agent talks to Nora's husband, Dan, about collateral. Dan owns an SUV that he says is worth at least $20,000. He offers the SUV as collateral.

Before he agrees to accept the SUV as collateral for Nora's bail, the bail agent must assess the value of the SUV. Dan says the value is $20,000, but the bail agent must determine whether this is the true worth of the vehicle.

Perhaps Dan doesn't really hold the title. The SUV might belong to his brother-in-law and Dan thinks he won't mind if he uses the vehicle as collateral. If that's the case, the bail agent cannot accept the vehicle as collateral. The cosigner must own whatever property is offered as collateral.

Validating the collateral can be as simple as photocopying the title certificate for the vehicle, along with a copy of the owner's driver's license or other official identification. When accepting a vehicle as collateral, a bail agent will often choose to perfect the title, which means he has the title signed over to him. After the defendant fulfills all of his obligations to the court, the bail agent will sign the title back over to the owner.

The collateral should be equal to or greater than the bail

amount. This doesn't refer to the purchase value of the item, but rather the value of the item if the bail agent is required to sell it for cash. Cars, boats and other vehicles lose their value each year after purchase, so it's important that the bail agent determine the actual current value. Dan's $20,000 SUV might not be worth that much any longer. It might be worth only $10,000 now. The approximate current value can be checked using the Kelly Blue Book, available online at http://www.kbb.com.

If a large bond is required, say $500,000 or higher, real estate will most likely be used as collateral. To assess the value of real estate collateral, the bail agent has to do some research. First he obtains information about the property from the cosigner. He then does a title search to be sure the cosigner really owns the property and that it is worth at least as much as the bail amount.

Title information is available at the county recorder's office, but that takes valuable time. To find the information faster, the bail agent can run a title search through a service such as Dataquick.com. Dataquick charges roughly $2-$5 per search and promises results in 10 seconds with as little information as the person's name and address. A trip to the county recorder might cost $5 just for parking, not to mention the drive time. The bail agent needs to perform the risk assessment and verify the property as quickly and efficiently as possible, because the defendant is waiting in jail. He might not wait too long before contacting another bail agent.

If the bail agent determines that the property offers sufficient collateral, he will fill out a deed of trust – also called a trust deed and assignment of rents. This is a legal document used to track ownership of a piece of property. The bail agent fills out the deed and has the property owner sign it. The deed must be notarized. After the document is filed at the county recorder's office, the bail agent is now on title to the property until the defendant meets all of his court requirements.

Jewelry is not commonly accepted as collateral for a bail bond. People often believe that an expensive ring can get them out of jail, because that's how the bail bond industry has been portrayed on television and in film. But jewelry is no longer used very often. Electronics can sometimes be used as collateral, but the resale value is not very high, so they don't serve as strong collateral.

Cash collateral is not used as commonly as real estate, but it is offered in some cases. Why would a person who has the full bail amount in cash hire a bail agent? Why wouldn't they simply pay the full bail amount at the court and save themselves the cost of the agent's fee?

There are some drawbacks to depositing large sums of money into the court system. The money will be tied up for three to four months after the case has ended, and the case itself might take a year or more to decide. If the defendant needs money for legal expenses or everyday living expenses for the duration of the case, he can't access the bail money he gave the courts.

A defendant who has deposited cash collateral with a bail agent has more flexibility. He can exchange one form of collateral for another. If he needs the cash to pay his attorney or for an unexpected emergency, he can then offer a different type of collateral. The bail agent will then return the cash to the client.

Another disadvantage to depositing cash in court is that if the defendant fails to appear, the court can confiscate the cash and never return it – even if the case is eventually dismissed. That decision depends on the judge's discretion. If the cash is deposited as collateral with a bail agent instead, the cash cannot be confiscated if the defendant eventually appears in court.

A bail agent might require cash collateral in some cases. For example, if a defendant lives in Texas but is arrested and brought into custody while vacationing in Florida, and the defendant's parents live in Texas, the bail agent might suspect that the defendant will skip town. If the bail amount is fairly low, e.g., $5,000, the agent will ask the parents for their credit card, cash or a bank wire transfer as collateral. Why?

If the bail agent posts a $5,000 bond for someone who lives out of state, the defendant might not have much incentive to return to resolve the case. The bail agent will incur expenses trying to get the defendant back to Florida to appear in court. Moreover, because the bail agent is licensed in Florida, he might not be familiar with Texas law and can encounter legal entanglements in trying to return the defendant to Florida. So while cash collateral is not used as often as other types, sometimes it's the better option.

After performing risk assessments, bail agents turn down anywhere from10-75% of callers. Larger bail agencies are willing to take more risks so they will turn down fewer bonds than smaller agencies. You'll find that many of the potential clients that call you are price shopping, while others are comparing collateral requirements among different agencies.

Posting bail and release of the defendant

If the bail agent and the cosigner come to an agreement on the collateral and the bail agent decides he will write the bond, they will make arrangements to meet. The meeting can take place anywhere that is convenient for the cosigner: The bail agent's office, the courthouse, a fast food restaurant, a parking lot, the cosigner's home or office, or most commonly at the jail.

As with all legal matters, bail bond processing involves paperwork. The bail agent prepares the paperwork in advance, and the cosigner signs everything when they meet. The paperwork usually includes a bail bond agreement in which the cosigner acknowledges he is responsible for ensuring that the defendant shows up in court.

Because many legal documents are long, complicated and wordy, the bail agent might also ask the cosigner to sign a "plain talk contract" – a brief document that explains in simple language the terms of the bail bond arrangement. Some surety companies also provide a checklist outlining the basic concepts the cosigner needs to be aware of.

The wording in a plain talk contract or checklist might be as follows:

> I understand I am responsible for paying the full amount of the bond posted if the defendant does not appear in court for every appearance and any other time ordered by the court until the defendant is sentenced or the case dismissed by the court. The court will enter a forfeiture of the bail if the defendant fails to make any court appearance. I understand that if the

> bond is ordered forfeited and it is not ordered reinstated or exonerated, that I must pay the full amount of the bail forfeited to the bail agency.

Compare that "plain talk" wording to the complicated legal language of the bond itself:

> BAIL COMPANY X hereby undertakes that the above-named defendant will appear in the above-named court on the date above set forth to answer any charge in any accusatory pleading based on the acts supporting the complaint filed against him/her and all duly authorized amendments thereof, in whatever court it may be prosecuted, and will at all times hold him/herself amenable to the orders and process of the court, and, if convicted, will appear for pronouncement of judgment or grant of probation.

Having the terms of the bond spelled out in plain language ensures all parties understand their responsibilities. Remember that many individuals who post bond are doing it for the first time. They are often in a state of panic or confusion about the process.

When cosigners meet with bail agents, they will need to supply the bail agent with the collateral if it is required at that time. The cosigner also pays the bail agent his fee. The bail agent then signs off on the paperwork and fills out the bond.

The bail bond is in two parts. The face sheet contains spaces where the bail agent fills in information such as the defendant's name, case number and first scheduled court appearance. The second part is the power of attorney, which must be attached in order for the bond to be valid. It contains the bond power and other legalese that gives the bond its authority.

Next, the bail agent takes the bond document to the jailer. The bond document is always physically delivered to the jail. It cannot be done over the telephone or via fax. Either the bail agent or the cosigner can deliver the paperwork. Increasingly, jails are requiring that the bond be delivered by a licensed bail agent who must show a copy of his license when the bond is delivered.

The jailer makes sure the information on the bond is correct – the spelling of the defendant's name, the charges and other pertinent information. The jailer then releases the defendant.

The paperwork isn't over yet. Once released, the defendant signs the same documents as the cosigner and fills out a detailed profile: the names and phone numbers of immediate family members, employment information and details about his vehicles, real estate and other assets. The bail agent needs to know the client as thoroughly as possible in case he needs to track down the client – or his assets – later. For the same reason, the bail agent usually takes a picture of the defendant – he might need to show it around town if the defendant skips bail.

Because many defendants are unfamiliar with the criminal justice system, the bail agent carefully explains the next steps to the defendant: when the defendant is scheduled to appear in court and how the defendant/cosigner will forfeit the items given as collateral if the defendant fails to show at the appointed date and time.

The bond doesn't cover only one court appearance. It is designed to ensure that the defendant is present at every hearing or trial date until the case is closed. The bond is renewable, so if the trial is still going on a year after it is issued, the bail agent can renew the bond and collect another 10% premium on the amount. Either way, the bond is still in effect throughout the case.

The initial meeting between the defendant and bail agent can be delayed if the defendant is held at a larger jail, where his release might take hours. In that case, most bail agents require that the defendant show up at the bail agent's office within 24 hours to complete the paperwork.

However, if the release is going to take less than an hour, it's best for the bail agent to wait for the release so he will have the information right away. At that point, the defendant will be very glad to see the bail agent and will be more cooperative about filling out anything the bail agent asks. Some jails give bail agents access to the defendant to fill out the paperwork while the defendant is still in custody, but that varies by jail.

All parties to the bail bond process retain some portion of the documentation for their records. The actual bond document becomes part of the defendant's file at the jail. That file is then forwarded to the court to prepare for the defendant's court appearance. The bail agent and surety company each retain a copy of the bond. The bail agent also keeps a copy of the "Power of Attorney Over Bond." The cosigner receives a receipt from the bail agent noting the fee paid, the court date, the charges and the location where the defendant needs to appear. Finally, there is a receipt for any collateral the bail agent receives from the cosigner. The cosigner and the bail agent both sign and date the receipt. When the collateral is returned at the end of the case, both parties sign and date the receipt again.

If all goes well, the defendant makes all his court appearances, the case is either dismissed or ended with a judgment of guilty or not guilty, and the bond is no longer needed because the defendant no longer needs to make any court appearances. The bond is cancelled (the term in the business is "exonerated"), and any collateral is returned to the defendant or cosigner.

A bail agent's fees

Although helping a fellow citizen in need is a rewarding experience, the bail agent can't earn a living on good feelings. He needs an income like everyone else. As soon as the defendant is released, the bail agent has accomplished the task he was hired to do. He receives his premium, or fee, that is a percentage of the total bail amount. This percentage is regulated by state law. In most cases it is 10%, although Nevada and Colorado allow 15%.

Some states have detailed regulations concerning bail agent fees. For example, in New York, bail agents can charge 10% on the first $3,000, 8% on amounts from $3,000 to $10,000, and 6% on the portion of the bond exceeding $10,000. Therefore, a bail agent's premium on a $100,000 bond is $6,260, not $10,000. Agents charging excessive fees in New York are fined $500 for each offense.

The collection of fees is trickier for bail agents than for

most business people. Bail agents have many one-time clients, so there's no chance to build trust with a client. There's also a greater chance that the bail agent's customer is an untrustworthy person, compared to the clients for other types of businesses. For these reasons, most bail agents require that their fees be paid up front.

Many bail agents accept credit card payments, but this requires extra precautions. Many defendants have attempted to pay their bail agent with stolen credit cards, so bail agents have to be on their toes. The bail agent must be sure:

- The card is a real card, not counterfeit.
- The card is current, not expired.
- The card belongs to the defendant and was not stolen.
- The account has the necessary available credit.

In order to accept credit card payments, a bail agent will need to sign up for credit card services (*see Chapter 5 – Starting Your Own Bail Bond Business*).

As a last resort, a bail agent may accept a personal check. As with credit cards, checks are often a risk. Defendants might try to pay with bad checks or even counterfeit checks – even though writing bad checks for large amounts is a felony. Usually, bail agents accept personal checks only from an individual who is likely concerned about his credit: perhaps a parent or grandparent of the defendant. A bail agent can call the bank from which the check is drawn to verify that the account is legitimate and contains the funds.

Whichever form of payment is accepted, the bail agent is responsible for verifying the funds. Sometimes people who seem sincere are not. That's why some bail agents prefer that their fees be paid in cash.

It's possible for bail agents to offer payment plans, so their clients don't need to pay their fees up front in full. This requires tracking payments and entails the risk that the remaining payments won't be made. Whether or not to offer payment plans is a matter of personal choice. Bail agents have to weigh the risk and extra work of a payment plan option against the extra customers that might be gained by offering this special service. Most people don't have an extra thousand dollars sitting around to bail out a friend, so payment plans often work out well in those cases.

Bail agents can also charge fees for travel, phones, collect calls, title searches, trust deed recording and posting. These additional fees are also regulated by state. On large bonds, most bail agents don't bother charging the additional expenses. The premium is high enough that the agent knows he will earn a good profit. On a $50,000 bond, for example, the bail agent is going to receive a premium of $5,000, so paying the cost of a few phone calls and a $10 computer search isn't going to result in a loss.

Bail agents are required to pay a percentage of their premium to the surety company that issues the bond – usually anywhere from 10-40%. The fees charged to the bail agent by the surety company are not regulated by the DOI. Therefore, the surety company is free to charge whatever rate they choose. Some surety companies also charge the client an administrative fee of $10-$15 per bond. This is a flat-rate fee, and part of it goes to the bail agent. On a $15 administrative fee, for example, the bail agent might receive $10 and the surety $5.

Let's say the bail agent has posted a bond for $20,000. His premium or fee would be 10%, or $2,000. His surety company charges a 15% fee on his premium to cover the cost of issuing the bond and to earn a profit, so the agent pays the surety company $300. The surety company also requires that 10% of the agent's premium go into the agent's BUF, which is discussed in detail in the next chapter. That's another $200. So the bail agent takes home $1,500. If the bail agent's surety company requires an administrative fee, he might receive an additional $10.

It's best that the bail agent not spend his fee until the case is over, as problems can arise. The bail agent might discover, for example, that the defendant has lied on one of the forms. Some defendants write down fake addresses or phone numbers for themselves or their family members. Sometimes they lie about their social security number, date of birth or driver's license number. All are justifiable reasons for the bail agent to revoke his promise to provide bail. People who lie about this type of information are deliberately trying to make themselves harder to locate if they skip town.

If the bail agent believes the defendant is going to leave town, he needs to revoke the bail bond. In that case, the collateral is returned and the defendant is re-arrested. Depending on the circumstances, the bail agent might have to return all or part of his fee. This means the bail agent has spent his time and money on the case without earning any income in return. Although this is not good for business, it's better than the alternative: the agent might spend even more time and money chasing a defendant who fails to appear. And the agent is saving the cosigner the cost of the bail amount should the defendant decide to skip.

If a bail agent doesn't return his fee in such a case and the cosigner wants the fee refunded, the bail agent might end up in court explaining to the judge why he had the defendant re-arrested. Therefore, bail agents should be careful in having a defendant re-arrested.

If the bail agent has a solid case, most likely the judge will not order a refund of the fee. For example, if the bail agent can prove the defendant lied or that the bail agent received a tip from someone saying the defendant had withdrawn all his money from his bank account, sold his belongings and bought a ticket to New Zealand, the judge will be sympathetic toward the bail agent. Judges want to see criminals in court, not in New Zealand.

A bail agent keeps his fee regardless of how a defendant's case progresses. If it's discovered later that the defendant was wrongly arrested, if the bail amount is later reduced or the charges are dropped, or if the defendant is eventually found innocent, the bail agent still keeps his fee. A lawyer still gets paid if the defendant is found innocent. Police officers are paid for their work on the case, regardless of the outcome. The same is true for bail agents, who completed their job of getting the client out of jail. Their services are actually all the more valuable when the person is innocent.

If the person is arrested for a new crime while out on bail – approximately 16% of released defendants are re-arrested for new crimes – the bond is not affected. The bond was made to ensure that the defendant appeared for all court dates involving his first crime. It doesn't ensure that he's not going to commit another crime.

However, a bail agent might not want to keep a client who's been re-arrested. The facts of the case have changed. The defendant might be more of a flight risk now because he is facing more charges. Let's say a man named Tom is arrested for driving drunk. He doesn't have much of a criminal history and didn't cause an accident, so he is released on a small bail bond. While he's waiting for his court appearance for the DUI, he commits a serious crime that carries a 25-year sentence if convicted.

This changes the facts of Tom's case substantially. He has much more at stake now. So does the bail agent who bailed him out on the DUI. The bail agent can go to the jail or courthouse and surrender Tom on the DUI case. This exonerates the bail agent's bond, and he is now free from any liability in this case. The bail agent keeps his fee for the bond, because it was Tom's actions that caused him to be placed back in jail and increased the risk and liability for the bail agent.

It's possible that the jail where Tom is taken might not even know he is out on bail for another crime. If Tom is allowed bail in his new case, he might call a different bail agent to try to get him out. If Tom manages to get released on bail before the initial bail agent is aware of the situation, the initial agent can go out and arrest Tom himself. The bail agent must then appear before the judge and explain why he arrested Tom and ask the judge to exonerate the bond for Tom's DUI.

The power of bail agents to arrest defendants varies from state to state. Usually the owner of a bail agency can arrest only those defendants for whom the agency has posted bond. This is obviously a legal matter, and you need to know the guidelines before arresting anyone.

Quick review of the bail bond process

Here's a summary of what happens from arrest to case closed:

1. **Defendant is arrested.** The defendant is arrested by a law enforcement agency and taken to the police station for booking or incarceration.
2. **Defendant calls attorney, family or friend for help.**
3. **Attorney, family member or friend calls bail agent.**
4. **Bail agent acquires collateral and a premium from defendant or co-signer and secures bond.** All necessary paperwork is completed.
5. **Bond is posted.** Bail agent visits jail and posts bond for the defendant's release.
6. **Defendant is released.** Court date is set.
7. **Defendant makes court appearance**. Defendant makes court date with or without attorney. Case is eventually decided.
8. **Collateral is released**. Bond is exonerated based on court appearance and court decision.
9. **File Closed.** Upon receiving notice of exoneration, the bail agent closes the defendant's file.

5

STARTING YOUR OWN BAIL BOND BUSINESS

Step 1: Obtain a license

The first step in starting your bail bond agency is to get licensed. Licensing requirements vary from state to state, and usually entail a one- or two-day course followed by an exam administered by the DOI. In some states, the industry is mildly regulated. In others, such as Nevada, it is closely regulated, with lengthy and detailed laws. Most states require a state license, but some require licenses at the county level instead (*see Appendix – Resources*).

Some states have more than one level of state licenses. The main license to be concerned about if you're starting your own business is the bail agent license, usually issued by the DOI, Bureau of Insurance or Department of Commerce in each state. A person usually must reside in the state he is licensed in, and the license must be renewed each year. There might be an annual fee attached – $25, $50 or $150 – in addition to any course or exam fees. Fingerprinting and background checks are being required by more and more states. Most states have licensing packets containing all the necessary paperwork and information, which can be requested by phone or by e-mail from the appropriate web sites.

California has three levels of licenses, including a solicitor's license for those who want to work for an existing bail company as an employee and don't want to write their own bonds. This license is the one to choose if you feel you lack the entrepreneurial spirit to run your own company or if you are just starting out and want to become familiar with the industry. If you want to eventually run your own business, you'll need experience in order to be appointed to a surety company. The solicitor's license is a good way to get that experience before setting out on your own.

Pre-licensing courses

Passing a licensing exam is not enough in most states. Bail agent candidates must also attend a pre-licensing course. At the end of the course, the candidate is given a certificate of completion that is good for one year. Candidates who have not taken the bail bond exam within one year of completing the pre-licensing course must retake the course. A candidate can't obtain a license without a valid certificate of completion even if he passes the exam.

The pre-licensing course can be taken either through the local bail association or an independent training center. The cost for this course in California ranges between $200 and $300, which covers the cost of the course and study material. It doesn't matter where a candidate attends the course. All the training facilities in a given state teach the same information.

The course is very helpful because it covers the material on the exam, making it easier to study for and pass the exam.

The exam

The exam is given throughout the year at various testing sites in each state. Candidates must first apply for the test through the DOI, which then schedules the exam date and notifies the candidate. Should the candidate miss the exam date, he will need to reapply.

Exam formats differ by state. In California, the exam contains 50 to 100 multiple-choice, true-or-false and fill-in-the-blank questions that must be answered within 90 minutes. In Ohio, candidates have one hour to answer 60 multiple-choice questions. There are no math problems to solve or essay questions to answer. The questions involve the ethics, rules and regulations that apply to bail agents in their particular state.

Candidates will be tested to be sure they understand the state licensing requirements and what bail agents are allowed to do in that state. Of even greater focus is what bail agents are *not* allowed to do. Questions frequently focus on prohibited conduct such as false advertising, misrepresentation, excessive fees and other illegal acts. Candidates may also be tested for their knowledge in these areas:

- Basic legal terms
- Contracts
- Types of bonds
- Jurisdiction

- Court procedures
- The bond process
- Bond forfeiture
- Duties of a bail agent

An increasing number of states are contracting with outside companies like Experior for agent testing, so the testing procedures and methods are becoming standardized.

Notification of exam results varies by state. In California, candidates are told within two weeks of taking the exam whether or not they passed. States with computerized testing systems provide the results much faster, sometimes the same day.

A passing score is usually 70%. Those who pass the exam will receive a photo identification card from the DOI, along with an official license, which must be displayed at the agent's place of business next to any other business licenses required by the state or county.

Candidates who fail can reapply and retake the exam, usually after 30 days, and they can continue to retake the exam as many times as they need to pass it. However, they'll be required to pay the exam fee each time.

The following checklist for the bail agent licensing process from the state of Ohio website is typical, although specifics vary from state to state:

1. Apply for your license:

■ Complete an electronic criminal background check using WebCheck. Results are returned within two days.

■ Or complete a criminal background check by obtaining and processing a Civilian Identification Fingerprint Form (blue form) available at any police department or sheriff's office. Submit this form, accompanied by a $15 processing fee to: The Ohio Bureau of Criminal Identification and Investigation, [address]. This method may take a few weeks to complete.

■ Complete the Surety Bail Bond Agent application (available online); submit application, any supporting materials, $150 license fee, and a $10 processing fee to [address.] Once you have been approved for licensure, you will be notified of your eligibility to test via e-mail, fax, or mail. You may then register and schedule your exam.

2. Prepare for your exam:

■ Take the Surety Bail Bond pre-licensing education course.

■ Find the outline for your exam (available online).

■ Use appropriate study materials.

■ Register for your exam:

Complete the Ohio exam registration form (available online).

File the exam registration by mail, fax, or phone.

3. Schedule your exam:

■ Schedule your exam by phone, fax or mail; you may test at any of five testing centers in Ohio; you may also make arrangements through Experior to take Ohio insurance exams at other locations nationwide.

4. Take your exam:

■ Bring government-issued photo identification.

■ Bring original, unaltered Course Completion Certificate (you will not be admitted to the exam without this item).

■ Arrive 10 minutes prior to appointment.

5. After your exam:

■ You will receive a temporary license at the testing center upon successfully passing the exam.

■ Your photo Surety Bail Bond license will be sent to you in the mail within 10 business days.

Continuing education

Bail agents in most states must attend continuing education courses to keep their licenses. These courses are provided by either the state bail bond association or an independent training facility. States have guidelines as to which courses are approved and which are not.

Though the continuing education courses will require some of your time, the good news is that you will not need to retake a licensing exam. Agents simply submit proof to the DOI that they attended a course. Proof is usually in the form of a certificate issued by the course provider.

As with all other aspects of the industry, continuing education course requirements differ by state. In California, for example, bail agents are required each year to take a one-day, six-hour continuing education course provided by the Bail Bond Association for the State of California. In Ohio, bail agents must complete 14 credits of continuing education every two years. In Arizona, agents must complete 20 hours within each licensing period.

Step 2: Set up your accounts

A bail bond agency is different from other types of businesses regarding bank accounts. Bail agents need at least three separate accounts: the business's main checking account, the reserve account (BUF) and a trust account. An optional account is a credit card merchant account.

Business checking account

This checking account is used for everyday cash flow. All fees and income are deposited into this account, and business expenses are paid from it. This account should be reconciled every month – it's important to know the correct balance at all times. The money in this account represents the growth of your company.

Many sole proprietors are tempted to use their personal checking accounts for their business transactions, because they file a standard 1040 tax return and aren't required to file separate corporate tax returns. However, it's a good idea to have a separate checking account for your business. That way, it will be easier to track tax-deductible business expenses and to keep more accurate business bookkeeping records. A new fax machine for your office is tax deductible, but a new toaster for your kitchen is not. It helps if you don't purchase them on the same receipt. With a separate business checking account and accurate bookkeeping, you will easily be able to monitor how well your business is performing.

Having separate accounts does not necessarily mean you need to open the business checking account under a business name. You can use your own name. However, if you want customers to make payments to your business name, you should open the account under that name to avoid any identity hassles at the bank. Most states will require you to have a business license, although some do not. In order to open a business bank account, the bank will need proof of your DBA ("Doing Business As") forms. These you will get when you choose a name for your business and file it in the local newspaper as a public notice.

Reserve account

In most states, surety companies require that bail agents place a percentage of their fees earned into a special reserve account or BUF. Monthly statements of all transactions for this account are copied to both the surety company and the bail agent. This money is used as collateral in case the bail agent has to forfeit a bond. If the bail agent is unable to collect on collateral in a particular case, then the surety company pays the court with money from the agent's BUF.

The bail agent can't spend this money. He's not allowed to invest the money or use it in his daily practice, and he can't draw funds from the account without the consent of the surety company. When the bail agent retires, however, the BUF can serve as a retirement account. At that time, if all the bonds written against the account are exonerated, any money in the account is returned to the bail agent.

The amount returned to the agent at the end of his career might be thousands or even a million dollars, depending on how long the agent was in business and how many bonds he wrote. If the bail agent conducts his business professionally and follows his proper training throughout his career, the surety company will rarely need to draw from the BUF and the agent will have a nice sum left over.

Knowing that the fund represents a retirement fund, bail agents can deposit even more money into the BUF than the surety company requires. But that's not particularly advisable. This account earns very little interest. As the bail agent earns additional income, he should probably meet with a financial consultant to determine the most appropriate ways to invest his retirement money to receive a higher return.

Most surety companies require that the BUF have an opening balance of $10,000 to $50,000 dollars. This means the BUF is the largest capital investment needed to start a bail bond business. The BUF is only necessary when a bail agent opens his own agency. If you plan to work for another firm, you do not need any start-up capital and you aren't required to open a BUF with a surety company.

Trust account

A bail bond business needs a third account, the trust account, which is simply a separate account at a regular bank. Surety companies require that bail bond agencies maintain this additional account. The trust account is used for a specific purpose: depositing cash collateral. This separate account reduces the chance that a bail agent will spend money that is not rightfully his.

If a cosigner pays cash collateral rather than offering an asset such as an automobile or real estate, the cash collateral cannot be mixed with the money the agent was given as a fee. It must be deposited into the trust account and held in a fiduciary capacity, meaning held in trust. The funds are to be used only if the defendant or cosigner does not meet his obligations. When the bail bond has been exonerated, the funds are returned.

Any money going into a trust account should be carefully documented to avoid legal or bookkeeping problems. You do not need to pay taxes on money that is being held as collateral. It does not represent income. The cosigner should be given a collateral receipt signed by both parties that specifies that a certain amount of money was received on a certain date to be held for collateral.

Once the bond has been exonerated, the cash collateral is returned either as cash or by check. The bail agent should also document this return transaction with a receipt signed by both the cosigner and the agent, so the cosigner can't claim the money wasn't returned. It is important to document everything when dealing with cash. There is no risk as long as everything is done properly.

Credit card merchant account

In addition to the three bank accounts, bail agents should seriously consider opening a credit card merchant account. This is an account set up with a credit card processing company, and it allows bail agents to accept credit card payments for their premiums. These credit card services charge a fee, but customers whose only asset is their credit card are going to be looking for a bail agent who accepts credit cards.

Bond amounts are sometimes pretty high, and people don't have that much cash sitting around. Credit cards are also useful for people who need to post bail on a weekend when banks are closed. A credit card payment is better than a personal check. The bail agent knows right away whether or not the credit card is good, because the credit card processing company provides that information instantly, any time of the day or night.

The only money required up front for credit card processing is the cost of the equipment, although most companies require the first month's fees in advance. You can purchase the electronic equipment for several hundred dollars, and some companies provide lease arrangements for monthly payments. Credit card services will usually charge a flat monthly service fee plus a percentage of each transaction. Some services might require an additional 10-cent or 25-cent fee per transaction. Each company offers different plans depending on the volume of charges a customer makes each month.

The credit card company will provide you with detailed statements each month showing the charges made and fees assessed, so you will have this information for your financial and tax records. Shop around to find a reliable credit card processor that offers the best plan for your situation. If you go to your favorite Internet search engine and type in "credit card merchant account," you will find an overwhelming list of choices.

Step 3: Set up your office and supplies

As a new bail agent, you'll need to set up your office right away so you'll be ready for business. First you need to decide whether to work from home or rent an office. Each has benefits and drawbacks.

A home office is more convenient. You can field calls in your pajamas. While you're waiting for calls to come in, you can be cleaning your garage or watching a game on television. A home office also costs less than commercial real estate – considerably less in some locations. Expenses for your home office space can even be deducted from your income taxes – this requires that certain criteria be met and that you file an extra tax form or two, so talk to your accountant or visit http://www.irs.gov for guidelines.

The main drawback to a home office is that clients can't visit you there. Well, they can, but you don't really want them to. Remember, there's a chance that some of your defendants will really be guilty of serious crimes. They don't need to know where you live, much less visit you at home. Even though most of your clients will be harmless, you don't want to do anything that puts you or your family in danger.

Renting commercial office space is helpful in several ways. An office away from home allows you to separate business from home life. At home, you will encounter distractions that interfere with the routine work required to maintain your business. It might be hard for you to complete a report to your surety company, for example, when the yard needs mowing, the television is on or the kids are playing in the house.

A separate office also allows clients to visit you at your

office. It's best to have an office located near a jail or courthouse. Offices in these locations often have sufficient walk-in clients to pay the office rent.

Even if you decide to rent an office, it is necessary to have some workspace at home. Calls come in 24 hours a day, and you will likely be sleeping at home and need to excuse yourself into another room so you don't wake anyone.

After you set up your office, you'll need somc supplies so that you can get to work immediately. Supplies for a bail agent's office not only include the usual office equipment – computer, phones, fax, copier – but also the forms needed to process bail bonds. We'll look at some of those forms next, and then we'll discuss the other necessary supplies.

Bond Powers and Bail Agreements

When you start your business, you will be supplied with all of the necessary paperwork from the surety company, such as bonds and bail agreements.

Bonds are the "blank checks" that you will deposit with the jail to secure the release of your clients. This is your guarantee to the court that your bail bond agency will pay the full amount of the bond if a defendant does not meet his obligations.

Each bond has a bond power, which is the maximum worth of the bond. Bond powers usually start at $7,500 and increase by increments as follows: $15,000, $30,000, $50,000, $100,000, $250,000 and $500,000. The bond power may go as high as $1 million. The bond power is printed directly on the bond, e.g., SHALL NOT EXCEED THE SUM OF SEVEN THOUSAND FIVE HUNDRED DOLLARS

$7,500.00.

Bail agreements and applications are exactly what they sound like. Agreements are for the cosigner and defendant to sign to guarantee they will pay the full amount of the bail if the defendant does not show up for court. The application is what the agent uses to determine the cosigner's worth and obtain information about the defendant. The application is extensive and asks for personal information from both the defendant and cosigner. This information will help the bail agent locate the defendant if he skips and determine what the cosigner is worth if the agent needs to pursue legal action.

The surety company will also supply trust deeds, plain talk contracts, receipt books, collateral receipts and other forms relevant to a particular state. Trust deeds are provided so that cosigners need only sign blank deeds rather than using their own deeds. These allow the surety company to file a lien on the cosigner's property to guarantee the bond. Plain talk contracts are forms that the cosigner must sign, acknowledging they understand everything they have signed and agree to everything in the contract. Receipt books are for receiving payments. Collateral receipts are given to cosigners when they deposit collateral with the bail agent.

Phones

Your phone is your business lifeline. To be successful in this business, you need a reliable phone system that includes all the available services: call waiting, caller ID, call forwarding, etc. Even if these services cost a little extra per month, you will need them and they will be worth the investment. The phone system is one of the more important investments when starting your bail bond agency. If your phone doesn't work properly, you will lose business.

You should set up a phone system with more than one line, and use call waiting, so you won't miss incoming calls. You'll need a reliable cell phone as well, so you can take calls when you're out of the office. You might want to consider designating one cell phone strictly for business use, so your friends aren't calling you on that phone and interrupting your business calls.

Remember, if you can't be reached 24 hours a day, your clients will go to your competitors. For this reason, you might also consider an answering service, which allows you to have a live person answer the phone at all times, whether you're already on two lines at once or at home asleep. You can instruct the answering service to contact you immediately when they receive a call from one of your clients.

Many bail agents pay extra for a toll-free number. It might provide that slight advantage over a competitor who doesn't have one. Cosigners calling from a pay phone in the jail lobby will more likely call a toll-free number. Toll-free numbers used to be designated as 800 numbers, but now 877, 888 and other prefixes are common, so it wouldn't hurt to write "toll free" next to the number on advertising and business cards.

You can get a toll-free number for as little as $5 a month plus the cost per call received. You don't need a separate phone line for your toll-free number. This number can be programmed to ring into any phone you choose – your office phone or cell phone, for example. Most jails do not allow inmates to make toll-free calls, so it's also a good idea to list your local phone number that defendants can call collect.

A pager is also a good backup option. If you have a receptionist or answering service, a pager allows you to be notified that a caller is waiting for your services. A pager can also be used to contact you while you're in court, if you don't have a cell phone with a silent option.

Other electronics

You need a computer with a printer and also a fax machine. You could try to get by without these items, but the time they save is well worth the initial investment. The printer will allow you to write letters using your computer, which you'll find much easier than using a typewriter.

The fax will allow you to take on clients you might otherwise have to pass up. You will inevitably have a cosigner call you from another state who needs to post bail for someone arrested in your locale. When this happens, if you agree to write the bond, you might want to fax the cosigners the paperwork to sign and they can pay by fax.

A copier is also useful, so you might consider a four-in-one printer, fax, copier and scanner. You won't be making hundreds of copies of a document, so you don't need a big expensive copier. Most often you'll be making one or two copies of documents for your files.

Your computer doesn't need to have all the bells and whistles, just enough memory and speed for word processing, surfing the Internet and running any special bail agent software you might buy. You also need a reliable Internet connection. Ideally, your fax line should be separate from your phone line so the crucial phone line isn't tied up by faxes, but if you don't have a DSL or cable connection for your computer, you could have the fax line sharing your computer dial-up to save money initially.

You also need a camera to take pictures of defendants. It can be a cheap 35mm camera – unless you want a more expensive one – a Polaroid camera that allows you to have the picture instantly (although the film is expensive) or a digital camera that allows you to upload the photos onto your computer. Having photographs of your defendants will help you track them down in case they skip.

If you have several employees, you might invest in two-way radios for instant communication. And of course there are other tempting electronic gadgets such as PDAs, but you can buy those items as you need them and can afford them.

Additional items

You should have a desk, a filing cabinet and the standard office supplies: pens, paper for the fax and printer, file folders, a stapler, etc. You also need knowledge of where all the courts and jails are, which will come naturally as you become familiar with the locations you serve. Many of the jails and courts are online or you can reference the local yellow pages. You will also need to tack your bail license to the wall in your office – most DOIs require that you display it prominently in your office.

Office help

It's nice to have an office assistant who can answer phones and handle all the filing and record keeping, but your ability to hire office help depends on your budget. Hourly wages for office help range from $6-$10 per hour for entry level, depending on responsibilities, and a lot of paperwork and responsibility is involved with having employees: payroll deductions, tax deposits to the IRS, Social Security and Medicare payments, insurance, including unemployment, liability and Workman's Comp, etc.

Additionally, most of the time you will be required to license your office assistants, so they can negotiate bail with your clients or at a minimum be competent to discuss bail matters with people who call in. Therefore, you need to balance the cost and responsibility of having employees with the extra clients they allow you to take on because of their assistance.

Step 4: Bring in clients

The key to bringing in clients and building your business is advertising. If potential clients in your market don't know you exist, you won't have any sales. It's that simple. Advertising is somewhat different for bail bond agencies than for other businesses. Other companies can send sales people out to pitch the company's services. However, it's illegal for you as a bail agent to send your sales people to the jailhouse to convince defendants they need your services.

You might need to give a sales pitch when a defendant or cosigner calls to inquire about bail. Maybe that person wants to "shop around" to get the best deal or to find out whether you are a trustworthy bail agent. At that point, however, most people just want to get out of jail, so it won't take much to sell them on your services.

A typical incoming call from a prospective client consists of answering the caller's questions and explaining how the bail bond process works. You will already need to be familiar with the jail the defendant is in. Most people that call never had to post bail for anyone before and have learned everything they know about bail agents from television and the movies. It is your job to comfort them and answer any questions they might have.

It's often helpful to direct the conversation in a "how to go about things" sort of way. For example: "When a person is booked into X jail, here is the best way to expedite the defendant's release." Don't be afraid to tell the cosigner what they need to do. Most likely, that's why they're calling you – because they don't know what to do.

Your initial conversation with the client can last anywhere from five to 30 minutes. The longer you are on the phone with the person, the more likely they will retain your services rather than calling another bail bond agency. It is always good to build a rapport with the client, even if you have to talk about something other than bail.

Bail agents who have a separate office for their business should use that to its full advertising potential, especially if it's located near a jail. The office should have a sign clearly stating the bail bond services available and the phone number. For offices not located near jails or courthouses, you will bring in only clients who live or work in the immediate area. Advertising is therefore critical.

Advertising requires that you find your target market, identify your demographics and flood the target area with your name and services. Following are six common methods of promoting bail services:

- Yellow pages
- Bus bench ads
- Billboards
- Business cards
- Local attorneys
- Internet

There's always television advertising, but usually that's reserved for large companies with satellite offices, not for start-up businesses. Television advertising requires a large budget, and you might get too much bang for your buck: a single bail agent can't handle the response from an entire television market. Newspaper advertising doesn't lend itself to bail bond advertising. So save your money for the advertising methods that will allow you to reach your target market effectively.

Yellow pages

The yellow pages are the bail industry's favorite advertising media. If you can afford only one method of advertising, this is it. A yellow pages ad has several benefits:

- The yellow pages can accommodate almost any size business and advertising budget.
- The area covered by the yellow pages can be tailored to meet the geographic area that best fits your business.
- Most people go to the yellow pages to find a service they have never used before.

Think about it: unless a person is a career criminal, he has probably never used a bail agent. Unless he has friends who have run into the need for a bail agent, it's unlikely he has ever heard someone say, "If you're ever in trouble, call so-and-so. He's a great bail agent." The newly incarcerated inmate doesn't know who to call to get him out of jail.

If he calls one of his friends for help, that friend probably won't know who to call either. So the friend will turn to the yellow pages, a time-tested source of phone numbers for business services people need unexpectedly. The majority of telephone calls received by a bail agent are from people who saw the bail agent's listing in the yellow pages.

There is a strategy to advertising in the yellow pages. Remember that you're most likely not the only bail agent in town. You need to stand out among your competitors. In the yellow pages, size matters. Buy the largest ad you can afford. Sure, it's more expensive, and money might be tight at first. But it's the single best investment you can make in your new business.

Use color in your ad to draw attention. This requires more money, but it will pay for itself. Have the ad placed as near to the front of the "bail" section as possible, with the largest letter size possible. The small ads at the back of the section are usually for shoppers looking to find the best deal or a specific kind of service.

Plan your ad carefully. Keep in mind that you can change your yellow pages ad only once a year when the new directory is published. Unlike newspaper ads, where you can change the size and information from day to day, you will have to live with your yellow pages listing for a long time.

Put as much information in the ad as possible: your location, toll-free and local phone numbers, business hours (preferably 24 hours) and the services you provide. Include information that distinguishes your ad from others. Look at your competitors' ads and try to create a better ad – one with your own flare. Some phrases that bail agents use to promote themselves include "Collateral is Negotiable," "Payment Plans Available" and "Open 25 hours." If you accept credit cards or provide other services that will make the client's life easier, be sure to indicate that information in your ad.

You also need to consider how much geographic area you would like to cover in your yellow pages advertising. Obviously, the more phone books you are in, the better the chance someone will see your ad. However, it will also cost you more money, and the listing may be published so far away that you may not be willing or able to make the drive to the jail.

It's best to start with your local phone book. Most communities now have more than one directory, as publishers compete for yellow pages advertising, so your money may be spent before you even cover your hometown. You can expand your advertising as your business expands.

In most cases, payment for the advertisement is made monthly and payment is not due until the book is printed and published. Pay close attention to your relationship with the phone book company. Some phone book companies may require up to six months of advertising fees in advance. They base their decision usually on your credit and how much you are spending. They also take into consideration your industry and any past experience with phone book advertising.

Billboards

The rates for billboard ads vary dramatically, depending on the location of the billboard. Most advertising companies offer discounts if you rent more than one billboard or have a contract spanning several months, rather than just one month. For example, one company in the Midwest offers one billboard for one month at $195 per month. That same billboard would cost $170 per month with a 12-month contract. If the company advertises on two billboards a year, each costs $145 per month. A similar billboard from an advertising company in an Eastern state runs $250 per month. In Los Angeles some billboards cost up to $25,000 per month for prime locations. Because billboard advertising can be costly, it's not recommended for a new start-up business.

The billboard ad fee is paid monthly. Some companies offer one price that includes the cost of printing while others have separate production charges. Production can become expensive if you want fancy artwork and pictures on the billboard. Again, look around to see what your competitors are doing and determine how your ad can make you stand out.

Billboards are big. You can't miss them. Take a drive down any major street or highway and you'll see how billboards can make your presence known. The billboard is the king of promoting name recognition in inner city and suburban advertising. As with yellow pages advertising, you need to make a decision about geography. Because of the services you offer, the best place to be known is near the police department, jail or courthouse. Some bail agents also advertise on billboards near their offices.

Because billboard advertising mainly promotes name

recognition, don't rely on it to bring in day-to-day business. It supplements your other advertising. For example, if a person passes a billboard with your name on it every day on his way to work, your name is more likely to catch his eye when he actually needs a bail agent and is flipping through the yellow pages to find the best one.

Because billboards target people who are driving, the ad needs to be concise. People will have only two or three seconds to see the billboard as they pass. So be brief: Your company's name, phone number and a catchy slogan are all that's needed.

Bus bench advertising

Bus bench ads are similar to billboards, only smaller. Like billboards, they help establish name recognition. You'll often see bus bench ads for bail agents around police departments and jailhouses. A bus bench ad placed in front of a jail is always a good idea. Clients assume you must be local to that jail and will call you because they want someone who can show up quickly to get their friend out of jail.

Bus bench ads are much less expensive than billboards, so you might want to start with a bench ad before moving up to a billboard. One California company, for example, offers bus bench ads at $110 per bench per month for a minimum order of five benches.

Business cards

As with any business, it's a good idea to have business cards printed. They are an inexpensive way to promote your business. Hand them out to everyone you know – friends, relatives, neighbors, acquaintances in your social club or church – just to let them know you're in the business. Anyone might need a bail agent. Your grandmother's next-door neighbor might forget to pay her traffic ticket and find herself under arrest.

Carry the cards with you everywhere. Always have a supply on hand. Although some people you encounter are not allowed to promote your services – jailers, for instance, can't hand out your cards for you – it's good to get your business cards in the hands of attorneys or other such players in the criminal justice system. Just keep in mind that there are rules about where you can solicit clients, and handing out your business cards in the wrong place could land you on the other side of the criminal justice system.

Most states have laws that do not allow you to pass out cards in the courthouse or jail or police departments. Many of these rules are set by the DOI in each state. You will learn these rules and regulations when you go through your pre-licensing study course.

Attorneys

Attorneys play an important role in referring clients to bail agents. When people are arrested, they often call an attorney first. If the attorney knows that a bail agent is reputable and reliable, he will refer his clients to that bail agent or call the agent on the client's behalf. Criminal attorneys are obviously the most useful source of clients for bail agents, but there may be situations in which a bail agent wants to establish a relationship with attorneys specializing in corporate law or personal injury.

The DOI prohibits bail agents and attorneys from advertising together. Also, because solicitation by bail clients is not permitted at courthouses, jailhouses or police departments, any professional relationship between an attorney and a bail agent must be established away from these locations.

Internet

The Internet is the most modern means of advertising for the bail agent. Everyone has access to the Internet, either in his home or at the local library. Some people spend hours on the Internet and do most of their information gathering there. You can use the Internet to promote your bail bond agency in several ways.

First, the Internet has its own yellow pages. The best Internet yellow pages are actually extensions of the printed publications put out by the major phone companies. For example, Yahoo Yellow Pages is connected to BellSouth, SuperPages.com is from Verizon and SmartPages.com is by SBC. You can ask about online advertising rates when you sign up for your regular listing in your local phone book.

Most of the online yellow pages offer a free basic listing, even if you're not in the paid publication. However, these listings are given low priority. In order to boost your visibility online, you need to pay for an advertising package that allows you to add logos, banners and preferred placement of your listing. On SmartPages, these extras range from $16 to $135 per month.

The Internet yellow pages still don't compare to print publications for advertising on a local scale. They won't bring you the same return on investment as other means of advertising, so you might not want to upgrade your free listings at first. However, the Internet yellow pages do give you an Internet presence without the cost of a website. A listing in the Internet yellow pages gives searchers your name, address, phone number and a map to your location. Most people will plug in their zip code and pull up a category, which makes your advertising localized.

The second way to advertise on the Internet is through legal sites or directories. These are not attorney sites. They are sites providing information about legal issues, listing laws or providing other legal references. Two such directories that focus on bail agents, attorneys and investigators are Bail.com and AboutBail.com. You can either be listed in an online directory or pay for an ad that lists your phone number. You can also obtain an ad that Internet surfers can click through to reach your website.

The third way to use the Internet to promote your business is to set up your own website and submit it to search engines, so that your website link comes up when someone searches for a bail agent in your area. This doesn't mean you have to hire an expensive web designer or pay an Internet provider to manage your website. Some of the large website companies that register your site name have forms you can fill out with the pertinent information, and the company's software automatically builds a simple web page for you. You can do that in 30 minutes.

Your website name (e.g., nameofyourcompany.com), called the domain name or web address, is going to cost you $10 to $20 a year depending on the domain service you use.

Some services register your domain name for free if you buy their hosting or web-building services.

Some established companies that offer web hosting are Tierranet (http://www.tierranet.com), which offers basic hosting for $14.95 per month, and ValueWeb (http://www.valueweb.net), which offers web hosting and web design software to create your page for $19.95 per month. However, companies such as these face growing competition from hundreds of other companies. Even the big Internet names like Yahoo are jumping on the hosting bandwagon, with Yahoo offering packages starting at $11.95.

A simple online search will yield a long list of companies willing to host your site for under $10. As with any contract, be sure you research the company before you buy into anything. Get recommendations from friends or co-workers about a company's reliability. If your site always goes down or your e-mail doesn't work properly, you didn't save any money going with the cheaper hosting company.

To locate your website, someone will type "bail bonds" in the search field of their Internet browser, and the search engine will locate all appropriate sites. Search engines use key words, so it's important that when you sign up to be included in a search engine, you specify words for your site related to the bail bond industry, such as "bail," "bail bond" and "get out of jail."

It takes up to three months to get published on search engines. Some of the most popular are Yahoo, Google, AltaVista, Hotbot, Lycos, Looksmart, and AOL. Yahoo is the second most popular search engine after Google. Being listed on Yahoo, which is a manually compiled directory, increases the chances that Google, a "crawler-based" (or automated) search engine, will pick up your site. A site listing on Yahoo costs $299 per year.

Looksmart.com powers many popular search engines like MSN.com. Beyond the $29 sign-up fee, the service charges on a per-click basis, which means your company pays 20 cents each time someone uses a Looksmart search engine and then clicks to your website. The minimum monthly budget is $20 for 100 clicks.

Signing up for a search engine listing with Overture (http://www.overture.com) also places your website in front of many Internet searchers. Overture requires a $50 minimum deposit, and you must spend at least $20 per month. The system works on a bid basis. Let's say you place a bid of 10 cents per click on the term "bail bond." If other bail agents bid 9 cents or less, your listing will appear first when someone searches for the term "bail bond." If another agent bids 11 cents or higher on that term, your listing will appear lower.

The cost for Internet advertising can range anywhere from $100 to $10,000 per month, depending on how many search engines you wish to be published in, how many options you sign up for with each one, how many websites you need hosted, and how many places you advertise.

Don't make the mistake of thinking that Internet advertising is a waste of time for a bail agent. While it's true that a person sitting in jail won't have access to the Internet, that person's friends and relatives do, so when they get the call and don't know what to do next, they will often turn to the Internet – especially younger people, who don't seem to realize information is available anywhere outside the Internet. They might type the words "bail bonds" in the search engine, and if your website – or a directory where your site link appears – is called up on that search, they will be calling you.

Keeping track

Advertising is expensive, and you want to get a return on every dollar you spend. Therefore, it's important to track the effectiveness of every ad. You need to know whether or not a particular ad or type of advertising brings in new clients, and how many. This is simple to determine. Each time you get a call, remember to ask where the defendant or cosigner found your telephone number. Make it a habit to do so. It takes only a few seconds.

You can keep track of the responses the old-fashioned way by scribbling them on the notes you maintain on this client. Or you can use the software programs created for bail agents, which includes a field in which the agent can note the advertising source for each call. If you're using Microsoft Access, create a field for advertising.

However, the software doesn't do any good unless the information is entered into it. At some point during the posting of bail, you need to ask the question and write the answer. One way to make this process automatic is to make it part of one of the documents filled out when the bond is being completed. That way, when defendants or cosigners complete the necessary forms, they provide the information concerning where and how they found your agency.

Tally up the responses after a month or so. If you didn't receive any clients from an ad, drop it. If an ad brought in just enough business to pay for itself, give it another month to see if there's an improvement. If a month passes with no improvement, drop that ad too. Advertisements should do more than pay for themselves. Because they add to the cost of your business, you need to see a financial gain from them.

6

RUNNING A BAIL BOND BUSINESS

As soon as your advertising draws in your first client, you will be running a bail bond business. Soon, other clients will follow. As each day passes, you'll gain experience in the various activities that make up the daily life of the bail agent.

Answering calls

The telephone is the bail agent's most important tool. Each time the bail agent's phone rings, someone needs help getting out of jail. The person calling is usually a friend or family member who will serve as a cosigner. This person is probably anxious or excitable and might want to ramble on about how his friend or relative is innocent. Keep in mind that these are people in a time of need who in many cases have never experienced a bail situation before. They might be confused, angry or sad.

It is always a good idea to direct the conversation toward how you can help them. This will keep them from lingering on the unfairness of the arrest or the distress they are feeling. Ask questions such as:

- When was the defendant arrested?
- Which jail is the defendant in?
- Do you know how much the bail is?
- Does the defendant work?
- Where does he live and with whom?
- Who is going to cosign for the defendant?

Cosigners typically ask the following questions of the bail agent:

- What do I need to do to get the defendant out of jail fast?
- How much does it cost?
- What collateral is accepted?

Be as friendly as possible. Treat callers with respect and dignity – do not talk to them as if they are criminals. Remember, the person you are talking to is not the person accused of a crime. The caller could be a doctor, accountant, plumber, actor, waiter or CEO of a large company. When you treat your clients with respect, you will have an advantage over bail agents who don't.

Sometimes the defendant will call. This usually happens when defendants have been in jail before and have used your services. Or they might get your name from a jail list. Many jails supply a list of local bail agents to inmates so they can call to make arrangements for bail. The defendant will call the bail agent and tell the agent what the bail amount is and that they have the 10% to cover the fees. They often know more about the bail system than a friend who might call.

Attorneys will sometimes call the bail agent, but obviously they don't need to ask questions, because they know the system. They will tell the bail agent they have a client who needs to be bailed out of jail. They will relay the relevant information, pass on the name and number of a cosigner and ask the agent to follow up. Sometimes they will call to tell the bail agent they gave their client the bail agent's phone number and to expect a call.

You need to answer the phone every time it rings. Voice mail doesn't work in this industry, because most people who call bail agents are in a hurry. If you were a defendant sitting in jail and found only an answering machine when you tried to call a bail agent, would you wait for the bail agent to call you back? No. You would move on to another bail agent. The yellow pages have plenty of other listings.

Taking calls is a 24-hour job. You can hire an answering service or have the office phones transferred to your cell phone, home phone or another employee. Some agents have calls transferred to their pager, but this is not recommended. If a client has to leave you a message and wait for you to call back, chances are that he will move on to call one of your competitors. Get a reliable cell phone and an answering service to assist you, until you can have your office staffed 24 hours.

Each time the phone rings with a bail request, that doesn't mean you will get a new client. Often you'll discover that the person calling for bail services doesn't have the money to pay your fee or the collateral to back up the bond. New bail agents might be discouraged by the number of clients they turn away. Remember that many of the callers are just shopping for price, collateral requirements, payment plans, etc. You will not get every client that calls, nor will you want every client. Be choosy about who you deal with, to ensure that you write only good bail.

Your goal is to not have to chase people by bailing everybody out of jail. You might turn away as much as 50-60% of the calls you receive. Keep in mind that the companies that never turn down any clients are the ones that go out of business within a few years, because they constantly have to pay expenses on forfeited bonds that were issued using poor judgment.

Obtaining bail information

The bail agent needs to gather the appropriate bail information for every bond he writes. After you receive the call from a client, you will typically need to call the records department at the jail to find out the defendant's booking number, the charges against him, the court in which he will need to appear and the bail amount. If the defendant is in jail under an arrest warrant, you will need to obtain the warrant case number and name of the court that issued it. You will then call the cosigner back as quickly as possible to convey the bail amount and the next steps in the process – paperwork, collateral, etc. – that will lead to the defendant's release.

The key is to get the bail information as quickly as possible. If you take too long to call the cosigner back, the cosigner might call another bail agent. Even after placing a phone call asking for help from a bail agent, the cosigner and the defendant are under no obligation to use that bail agent's services. They can call several agents and use the services of the first one who takes action. No one wants to wait around in a jail cell.

A few jails and police departments have booking information on the Internet for faster access by bail agents. This might be the trend of the future. However, because the systems are often new, it's best to call the department to confirm the information.

Posting bonds

Timing is important throughout the bail process, not just after the initial call. When you set an appointment time with a cosigner, you need to arrive on time or even early. Bail agents have lost clients even when they show up on time, simply because there was another agent already at the jail who offered to take care of the bond right away.

The time it takes to receive a call and meet with a client depends mostly on the client. If you wait for the client to come to your office, you will be able to prepare for him. If you are taking real property as collateral, you will be able to research the property on the Internet before the client arrives at your office. If you are using a title to a car, you will need to wait until the client brings the title to your office, at which point you can complete all the paperwork.

If you plan to meet your client at the jail, you will need to allow 30-60 minutes to complete the paperwork before you leave for the meeting. If clients are calling from home, as most are, it could take them that long to arrive at the jail. If they live closer to the jail than you are, you might not have sufficient time to prepare. This is one reason having an office near the jail is helpful. This is also why advertising outside your locale can cause logistical problems. You will need the ability to get to the jail in a timely manner.

A bail agent wants to be able to serve as many clients as possible and should minimize travel time. If a defendant is held at a jail hours away and the amount of the bond is small, you might want to refuse the case or refer the defendant to a bail agent who works closer to that jail. If the bail amount is sizable, it might be worth the drive. You have to make a judgment call: Is the bond worth it? Do I need the new business? Do I even have time to drive to that jail?

Time can also be wasted by clerical errors. If the bail bond is not completed correctly, the jail will not accept it. Some will allow corrections to be written on the original bond, but many require an entirely new bond. This takes time not only in generating the new bond, but also in completing the paperwork for the surety company to account for the voided bonds. You aren't paid extra for spending this extra time, so it's important to avoid such errors.

Time-wasting errors can involve listing the wrong bail amount or the wrong date, but the most significant error involves the bond power. The defendant's bail amount cannot exceed the bond power listed on the bond that the bail agent presents. For example, if the bail amount is $7,501, then a $7,500 bond can't be used. However, any increment higher than that amount could be used. If a bail agent makes an error in the bond power, he must write out a new bond of the appropriate power, which will waste a few more minutes at the jail. It's always a good idea to take an extra bond to the jail in case such an error occurs, so that extra time is not wasted in going back to the office to get another blank bond.

Posting a bond requires that the completed paperwork be delivered to the jail for the defendant's release. In larger jails, the bond is delivered to the records clerk or cashier. The clerk will check that the bond is filled out correctly and process the bond for the defendant's release. The defendant's release can take anywhere from five minutes to several hours after the bond has been posted, depending on the size of the jail. Most large county jails take several hours to release an inmate.

As a bail agent, you do not need to wait for the defendant to be released from jail. If the jail is small, however, and the defendant will be released within 30 minutes, it's a good idea for you to wait. It is always beneficial to meet the defendant, to get a feel for what he is like in person and to gather as much information as you can about him while you have him there.

Although most bonds are posted at the jail, some are posted at the courthouse. When a defendant is in a jail, the bond will need to be deposited at that jail. When the defendant is in custody at a courthouse or walked into court on his own and was arrested, the bond will need to be deposited at the courthouse.

For example, when a defendant has a warrant for his arrest and decides to turn himself in, he is put in jail, and his attorney will have the defendant's name put "on calendar," which means the defendant is scheduled to appear in court. The attorney will call the bail agent to inform him of the scheduled appearance. On the court date, the defendant will show up with the attorney, who will ask for the defendant to be released on his own recognizance. If the judge refuses, the attorney will then ask for bail. If bail is granted, the bond is posted at that time.

In some courthouses, the bond can be posted with the court clerk sitting next to the judge. The clerk will check the bond to be sure it has been completed correctly before the defendant is released. Other courts have a bond clerk, whose specific job is handling every bond posted at that courthouse. The bond clerk is usually located in an office elsewhere in the courthouse, not in the courtroom. The bail agent must leave the courtroom, find the bond clerk and deliver the bond. After the bond has been reviewed and confirmed to be correct, it is sent back to the courtroom so the defendant can be released.

Collateral

When real property is used as collateral, the bail agent needs to decide whether to file a lien against the property. A lien doesn't claim ownership of the property. It is a charge against the property that indicates to everyone involved that there is a debt to be satisfied regarding the property – a debt that might require the sale of the property in order to be settled. The lien is for the bail amount and helps to guarantee the agent will be able to get money from the property if the defendant skips.

If the defendant seems solid, you might decide not to file the lien. He might simply have the property owner sign and notarize the deed of trust and not file it. Most often, however, you will take the deed of trust and file it with the county recorder's office, placing the lien against the house. If you have a deed of trust that isn't filed, the cosigners can sell the house without your awareness. This puts you in a situation of liability for the full bond amount with no collateral.

Filing a lien means completing the necessary documents, writing a check to the county recorder's office – the fee typically ranges from $10 to $24 – and recording the deed, either by personally delivering the lien paperwork or mailing it.

When the case is over and the bond is exonerated, you can remove the lien through the county recorder's office. It is very important not to remove the lien until you have proof the bond is exonerated. Don't just take the defendant's word for it if he calls and says the case is over.

A similar process is involved when cars are used as collateral. If you trust the defendant and cosigner, you might just hold the pink slip. If you're unsure about the case, you can decide to hold the pink slip and transfer the car into your name or the name of your bail bond agency. Otherwise, the title will remain in the cosigner's name. If that person is untrustworthy, he might go to the DMV and say he lost the title and have a new title issued. This would allow him to sell the car without your knowledge.

Posting transfer bonds

Another part of life for a bail agent is transfer bonds. They are used for posting bail for someone out of your area. You don't want to turn down business when your phone rings, so knowing how to use transfer bonds will help widen your client base.

The transfer bond process works as follows: If a bail agent in Los Angeles gets a call from someone in Los Angeles who has a friend or family member in jail in San Francisco, the bail agent contacts the San Francisco jail and gets all the necessary information as he normally would. He then calls his surety company, which will have one of its agents in San Francisco post the bond. This is called a transfer bond.

In a transfer bond situation, all standard fees and liabilities belong to the primary bail agent – the Los Angeles agent in the example above. However, the remote bail agent – in this case, the San Francisco agent – will typically receive a $50-$100 fee for posting the transfer bond. The primary bail agent can charge his client this extra fee, which is paid to the surety company along with the other bond costs. The surety company then pays the remote bail agent his $50-$100 fee. The primary bail agent signs a "Hold Harmless Agreement" stating that the remote agent will not be responsible for the defendant or the bond if the defendant should skip.

A bail agent may need to use transfer bonds only a few times a year, but these transfer bonds help him take advantage of every possible business opportunity. Along with gaining business as a primary agent on a transfer bond, the agent can also earn a little money by posting transfer bonds on behalf of an agent in another city.

Transfer bonds have a drawback, however. If the remote agent is busy with his own business, the $100 fee won't be as important as the potential $1,000 fee for the bond he is working on when he gets the call asking for the transfer bond. The transfer bond will be low priority and might not be completed until he finishes his other work. When a bond takes too long to execute, it reflects poorly on the primary bail agent, because his defendant is sitting in jail, counting the minutes until he is released. The cosigner might decide to call another bail agent who can get the job done faster.

To assure the transfer bond has been posted, it is a good idea to call the jail and ask if they have received the bond. Another way is to ask the surety company to obtain the bond number that the posting agent is using to post the bond. This might make the posting agent feel more obligated to complete the process a little quicker.

When a transfer bond situation arises, if the primary bail agent's surety company doesn't have an agent in the area in question, it will contact another surety company that does. The bail agent signs a "Hold Harmless Agreement" and the bond is posted in the same manner. Bonds can even be transferred out of state. The fee for the remote bail agent in an out-of-state bond transfer is typically \$100-\$300, which can be added on to the client's fee.

Following up on clients

Bail agents don't typically check up on every client who is out on bail. Often they rely on intuition. If something feels wrong or they don't trust the client, they might call the client regularly. Some bail agents require that a defendant check in with them every week. Others have defendants check in after every court date.

The most common personal information for a defendant to lie about is the phone number at which he can be contacted. This is usually your first indication that something is wrong. If you try to get in touch with a client but the client can't be reached or the phone numbers are false, that's a sign the defendant wasn't honest about his contact information – and probably won't be honest about keeping the terms of the bond.

If you reach a fake or wrong number, you can call the cosigner to try and reach the defendant. If that doesn't work, you have a list of contact information for the defendant's family members taken from the initial paperwork. If no one on this list is helpful, you can visit the address provided by the defendant or hire an investigator to check up on the defendant.

Or, you can show up for the first court date. If the defendant appears, you can surrender him back into custody, because at this point the defendant's dishonest and elusive behavior has made him too much of a risk. The bond would be exonerated and your risk would be ended. You will most often keep the entire fee you collected, although some judges have been known to require the bail agent to return a partial premium to the client. You should always have a good reason for arresting and surrendering defendants back into custody.

Paperwork and filing

Bail agents do not have a shortage of paperwork. Even as the criminal justice system becomes more electronic, paperwork and filing remain critical to the bail bond business. Therefore, you need a good filing system.

Each case involves paperwork. A simple case involves the most basic documents needed to create the bond, but more complex cases involving collateral will require paperwork pertaining to liens, property titles, etc. Some documents – such as the form that contains the defendant's contact information – are crucial and can't be lost.

As soon as you decide to post bail for a client, you should grab a legal size manila folder and start a file. Of course, it doesn't have to be a manila folder; you can use a green hanging file folder or a bright purple plastic folder. But basic manila folders are inexpensive and serve the purpose well. Assign a file number to the case to allow you to reference it quickly – this is particularly important if you have a computerized system.

The most important paperwork that a bail agent will file is his copy of the bond. Remember, there are three copies of the bond: one for the jailer, one for the surety company and one for your files.

Paperwork related to collateral is also critical: deeds of trust, lien paperwork, collateral receipts, etc. Sometimes a bail agent will have cosigners sign Disclosure Statements that indicate they understand what they are doing and know the risks of putting their property up as collateral. If collateral is a car or other vehicle, the bail agent's file will also contain the title to the vehicle and/or a bill of sale – documents necessary to enable you to sell the vehicle should the need arise.

In the file you open on each client, you will also include the bail bond application and any plain talk contracts or other forms the cosigner filled out. You might also have notes jotted down during your various phone conversations with the cosigner or defendant. If a transfer bond was used, a copy of the Hold Harmless Agreement from the surety company is also kept in the file.

You can find software specifically designed for the tasks performed by bail agents. It tracks all the pertinent information on filed documents. Once the information is entered into the computer, it can be accessed more quickly than using paper files. Some functions serve the same purpose as the paper files: the software allows you to maintain all of the defendant's information, such as collateral and personal information. The software can also store photos taken of the defendant and of any collateral. The photos are taken by a digital camera or scanned into a graphics file.

Some of the software programs perform functions that go beyond a simple paper file. A bail agent can track any outstanding fees or balances due them. The software also provides useful reports that can help with business management, such as average size bond, total bail written, total money earned and the number of bonds written per month. Some software programs provide form letters for common correspondence, and the bail agent needs only to insert his name into the form document rather than creating a new document from scratch.

If you type "bail bond software" into a search engine, you will get a list of companies that offer this type of software, including:

- Creative Software Solutions (http://www.bailbondsoftware.com)
- Sentry Link, producers of Bail Credit (http://www.sentrylink.com)
- Bail Tracker 2000 by National Surety Services (http://www.bailbonding.com/software)
- BailBond Professional by Trackum Software (http://www.bondsmansoftware.com)

Be sure to find out how long a company has been in business and ask for some testimonials before investing in software. You don't want to find yourself without technical support when the business goes under after a few months. Bail bond software products range in reliability and features, so ask if you can see a demo to evaluate the software before you purchase it.

Some companies provide these software services online. This means that the software is accessed over the Internet and the data is keep offsite. This is helpful in the event of a fire or computer theft, because the records are kept safe. However, if you don't have a reliable, high-speed Internet connection, these online services aren't very practical.

The cost of software can range from $500 to several thousand, depending on the features, such as multi-user capabilities for networks or support and upgrade agreements. If you just want a good database to track client information, you can use a program like Microsoft Access, which allows you to perform many of the same tasks as the specialized bail bonding software. You have to do a little more setup work, but if you're familiar with basic databases, Access might be all you need.

The availability of high-tech options doesn't mean you can toss out the low-tech file folder. You still need to keep the real documents. But a computer is faster at accessing one piece of information from a client's file, and if you have software, you only need to use the file folder when you want to view the original documents or you need to present them to someone.

Although software can make life easier, the bail agent has

to do his part by updating the computer files daily. Falling behind on data entry will lead to inaccurate or disorganized records, which defeats the purpose of having software. Entering information into a computer software program in a timely manner reinforces the filing process and helps you stay organized and in control of all your cases. Even if you are only posting one bond per day, it is better to enter one file daily than to wait until the end of the month and have to enter 30.

As a bail agent, you will have many cases going at once. Just because you have posted a bond for a client, that doesn't mean the case is over. It is likely that the case will continue for three to six months. This means that on any given day, you will be bailing someone out of jail and checking on past clients you posted bail for three months prior. This can make for a busy schedule if you are not organized.

A good filing system will make you faster and more efficient, reducing the possibility of mistakes or delays. A poor filing system might cost you not only time, but money as well. If you don't have an organized filing system, you might lose track of which clients owe you money and how much. You don't want to work for nothing. Also, if the court notifies you that a defendant failed to appear, you need quick access to that client's paperwork. If you lose that file, you might lose any chance of locating the defendant. In the end, it could cost you the amount of the bond.

In California, bail agents are required to keep their files for five years, but it's a good idea to keep them as long as possible for future reference. For instance, if you post bail for someone today who says he knows someone who used your services six years ago, that old file might serve as a good reference tool if this current client skips town.

Your files also provide a record of clients to avoid – clients who skipped bail the first time or still owe money for services. Conversely, if a past client forgot that he previously used your services and still owes money on an earlier case, it's easier to collect the remaining balance on the first case once the new bond is written, because you will have the defendant's new contact information, and the defendant will probably want to stay in your good graces until the case is over.

Tracking exonerations

Exonerations are key to ending the bail agent's legal and financial obligation to the courts. The word "exonerate" means to free from blame or responsibility. In the bail industry, this doesn't necessarily mean that the defendant has been exonerated of the crime of which he is accused. It means that the conditions of the bond have been fulfilled – the defendant has shown up for all court appearances and now the case has ended either with the defendant's release or incarceration. It means the bail agent is free from responsibility on that bond.

To exonerate the bond, the judge will say in open court, "For the record, bail bond is exonerated" and might announce the bond number. The bail agent is rarely in the courtroom when exoneration occurs. To certify the bond has been exonerated, the court stamps the bond with its seal and the words "Exonerated." Some courts automatically send a copy of the exonerated bond to the bail agent and surety company.

Because the court is bogged down processing the hundreds of other pieces of paper involved with each case, this process can take from one to two months. Some courts don't mail out exonerations at all. Because having a posted bond outstanding can be a stressful experience for the bail agent, he doesn't want to sit around in limbo, constantly wondering if he's going to have to come up with a $50,000 bond.

The bail agent should keep track, therefore, of all court dates for defendants he has bailed out. The first court date is already set when the defendant is released on bail and is written on the bond papers. One or two days after the court date, the bail agent should call the court clerk and ask if the case was settled. If not, he should ask about any new court dates.

These new court dates should be written in the client's file or entered into the bail agent's software, which can provide a report of pending court dates. Tracking court dates is tedious but necessary. If a defendant skips town, the bail agent can take action immediately and has a better chance of locating the defendant.

If you are not keeping track of the defendants you are worried about appearing, you might get burned. If the defendant fails to appear and you have not kept on top of the process, it is likely you will not be informed for up to 30 days. When you go to look for this defendant, he already has a 30-day head start. It is always beneficial to require that your defendants call you every week or after every court date, to update you on the progress of their case. This can save you from many headaches in the future.

The most uncertain time for a bail agent is once a defendant has been found guilty and is free on bail while awaiting sentencing. Up to this point, the defendant probably hoped he would be found not guilty or the case would be thrown out. Now the defendant faces certain punishment and is more likely to skip.

This is why a reliable cosigner and good collateral are important for cases in which defendants face jail or prison time. A bail agent can sleep better at night knowing that the cosigner is going to try and keep tabs on the defendant, and that even if the defendant skips, the bail agent has solid collateral to pay the forfeited bond.

If the court tells the bail agent that the bond was exonerated, he's still going to want a piece of paper that certifies the exoneration. If the court doesn't send this document automatically, the bail agent can request exoneration by mail by sending in a completed Certificate of Discharge form. Most surety companies will supply bail agents with these forms. The form contains the defendant's name, case number, bond number and the date the bond was written. The bail agent will receive a faster reply if he includes a self-addressed stamped envelope. Once the exoneration document is received from the court, the bail agent files it away and the account is closed.

Notarizing documents

Because bail agents are involved with many legal documents, they can save time and money by becoming notaries. Usually notaries are certified at the state level. In some states, the process is as simple as filling out an application, paying a fee and taking an oath.

Other states have stricter requirements. Applicants in Pennsylvania must obtain the endorsement of a state senator and two reputable citizens, along with taking a three-hour class and posting a $10,000 bond. The application fee in Pennsylvania is $40. In California, applicants must pass an exam, submit their fingerprints, pay a $40 fee and post a $15,000 bond. In Texas, the fee is $21 and the only requirements are that applicants must be legal Texas residents who have never been convicted of a felony or crime of "moral turpitude" – usually interpreted as a crime that is dishonest or vile to a high degree but can include common crimes such as forgery and bribery. A $10,000 bond is also required.

Along with helping your bail bond business work more efficiently, doing notary work on the side can provide a nice supplement to your income. People encounter all sorts of applications or contracts where their signatures need to be notarized, and you can provide this service quickly and easily. For more information, contact the National Notary Association (http://www.nationalnotary.org or toll free at 800-876-6827) or the United States Notary Association (http://www.enotary.org or toll free at 800-587-2588).

Accounting

In a business that revolves around money, it's important to keep track of every dollar. A bail bond agency can reap some benefits by hiring an accountant or bookkeeper. The main benefit is regular maintenance of the business books. The books will be up to date and reconciled with accurate information on a daily, weekly or monthly basis. The more business the bail agent has, the more frequently the books should be maintained.

Hiring an outside professional of course adds another expense to the business. Some bail agents choose, therefore, to maintain their own accounting books. This is a personal decision that you should base on your company's income and your familiarity with accounting principles.

Accounting Option 1: Hire someone to do the books

Companies that require audited financial statements for reporting to shareholders about their publicly traded shares of stock often hire certified public accountants or CPAs. So do companies that have big loans and are required to report their financial activity to the bank as part of the loan requirements.

A typical bail agent does not require audited statements and probably doesn't need a CPA. The Financial Accounting Standards Board of the American Institute of Certified Public Accountants doesn't have any specialized practices or procedures for the bail industry. Therefore, maintaining a proper set of books requires only a competent bookkeeper or accountant, as most bail agents require only sufficient financial records to file their income tax returns to the IRS. A bookkeeper can maintain the agency's books at the level needed to prepare the agent's federal, state and local tax returns and can create the two financial statements most important for managing the business: the profit and loss (P&L) statement and the balance sheet.

The P&L shows the company's financial performance, measured as revenue (or profit) minus expenses (or loss), over a specified period of time. You can create a P&L for each year for your income taxes, or for a particular month so you can compare your income to the previous month. The P&L is a key indicator of how the company is performing financially.

The balance sheet shows how much money the company has at any given point in time, usually stated monthly or at the end of the year, and indicates what the business is worth on the day the report is generated. In addition to keeping a bail agent informed about how his business is performing, these financial statements are used to prepare tax returns. The balance sheet takes into account the owner's assets, such as money in bank accounts, minus any money the bail agent owes. Liability on a bond doesn't count on the balance sheet unless the defendant skips.

Another accounting principle a bail agent will need to learn is the difference between cash and accrual bookkeeping. Cash bookkeeping means you track money as you receive it and as you spend it. The accrual system tracks money as soon as it is owed to you or by you. For example, if you send a bill for $1,000 to a client, you are owed that money from that moment on. In accrual accounting, that amount would be posted immediately to your income. But you don't have that $1,000 yet. In cash accounting, you do not count that income until you have the cash (or check representing cash) in your hand.

Accrual-basis reporting helps if you are trying to maximize revenue. Perhaps you want to apply for a bank loan. You have invoiced clients for $10,000 that hasn't been paid yet. Your financial statements will look better to the bank if they are created using accrual accounting, because the $10,000 is presented as income. Cash-basis reporting is useful when you are trying to minimize revenue, mainly for tax reporting when you have to pay income taxes based on total income.

Most bail agents maintain their books on a cash basis because they use their books only for filing tax returns and have no need to maintain an accrual set of books. Furthermore, the bail business doesn't operate similar to other businesses in terms of fee payment. In other businesses, clients might be sent an invoice and are given 30 days to pay. Sometimes the customer might be late in paying. A bail agency usually requires fees up front or within a few days of posting the bond. Reporting unearned income for such a short period of time is immaterial, making cash-basis accounting the only practical way to maintain books for a bail bond business.

Even if a bail agent hires someone else to keep the books, the bail agent still plays a role in the bookkeeping process. He must record all financial transactions and turn over the records supporting those transactions – bank statements, check stubs, invoices, check payments received, etc. – to the bookkeeper.

Accounting Option 2: Do your own accounting

Because most bail agencies are small businesses operating as sole proprietorships, bail agents can opt to maintain their own accounts using ledger books or any of the popular consumer accounting software, such as QuickBooks or Peachtree, available at most office supply or electronics stores. This software does most of the bookkeeping automatically. It also generates detailed reports at the touch of a button, creates pie charts for expenses and income, and prints professional check registers or invoices.

However, it's helpful if you understand the concepts behind these reports and graphs. You should know a little about basic accounting. You can gain that knowledge by attending a basic accounting or bookkeeping course at a local community college, by buying or borrowing one of the many books that explain accounting principles in simple terms, or by visiting a good instructional site on the Internet.

Accounting software depends on the information you enter on a regular basis. If you billed someone for expenses and that person paid the bill, for example, you need to enter the payment into your accounting program. Otherwise, when you print out a report to show who owes you money, that person will still be listed on the report even though the bill was paid.

Most bail agents are self-employed entrepreneurs who are busy generating and serving new clients and have little time to maintain accounting software. This defeats the purpose of having the software in the first place. Some of the bail bond software programs provide accounting features. If you will be doing your own accounting, this industry-specific software might be a better choice.

All of these activities make up the typical day for a bail agent. It's an unpredictable business. You might be busy posting bail for three days straight because of some law enforcement crackdown. Then your phone might not ring for the next three days. When you're not posting bonds, you should always use your down time to catch up on paperwork, accounting and other business management activities, because you never know when your phone will start ringing off the hook.

Most bail agents will tell you that the holidays are a busy time for them, particularly November through December. Also, hot summer days usually bring about more arrests than cold winter days, so summer is usually a busier time for bail agents in general. Although weekends may bring a few more arrests because people are partying or have extra time on their hands, bail agents don't have any court-related work to do on weekends, as courts aren't in session. Therefore, the work evens out over the course of a week.

The bottom line is that you never know what to expect. Be prepared to take on cases at a moment's notice, but budget your money in case you don't.

7

WHEN THINGS GO WRONG

A golfer knows it's going to be a bad day when he wakes up to a rainy sky. A manufacturer knows it's going to be a bad day when he comes to work and is greeted by picket signs. A bail agent knows it might be a bad day when he receives a notice from the court saying a defendant didn't appear on the designated date and time. At this point, the bail agent has to worry that the defendant has become a "skip" – a defendant who has absconded, which means he has secretly slipped out of town to avoid prosecution.

When a skip absconds, the bail agent has a limited time to locate the defendant before being held responsible for the full bail amount and having to pay off the bond. The time limit to locate a defendant varies from state to state. It's 180 days in California. Bail agents in Pennsylvania have only 20 days, while those in Florida have 60. If the defendant isn't located, the bond will be in forfeit; because the defendant or cosigner didn't meet the conditions of the bond agreement, the full bond amount must be paid. The court will also issue a bench warrant, which means that any law enforcement officer who encounters the defendant should arrest him.

Skip and a jump

When the bail agent receives the notification from the court that the defendant failed to appear, he calls the court to be sure the defendant didn't re-appear or report to the court later. Sometimes defendants don't appear at the right time because of a miscommunication or because they forgot. If the defendant hasn't re-appeared, the bail agent checks the jails to see if the defendant has been re-arrested for a different crime. If not, the bail agent contacts the cosigner, asking why the defendant failed to appear.

If the cosigner is cooperative, the bail agent might give him a few days to locate the defendant. If the cosigner does not know where the defendant is but wants to cooperate and wants the bail agent to arrest the defendant, he will need to supply the bail agent with as much information as possible about the defendant to assist in arresting him. If the cosigner refuses to cooperate and knows but won't reveal the defendant's whereabouts, the bail agent knows the case won't be easy. At this point, he either has to look for the defendant himself or hire a bail enforcement agent (BEA), a specialized private investigator commonly known as a bounty hunter, to locate the defendant. Unfortunately this means the bail agent will also be saddled with investigative expenses.

If the bail agent hires a BEA, he can expect to pay anywhere from 10-20% of the bail amount plus the BEA's expenses. On a $10,000 bond, for example, a BEA will charge a fee of 10-20%, or $1,000-$2,000, plus any expenses he incurs in the investigation. The BEA will charge the bail agent directly. The bail agent can legally pass the BEA's fees to the cosigner, but it's up to the bail agent to collect the fees.

This is where some of the paperwork signed earlier comes into play. A good bond agreement includes a clause stating that the cosigner will pay the costs involved in locating a missing defendant. The rates for a bail agent's time for investigative expenses are usually spelled out in the original bond agreement. Even though it's in the best interest of the cosigner to locate the defendant quickly, in order not to forfeit the collateral and incur investigative expenses, all of the terms need to be in writing before the bond is posted. It's an unfortunate reality that of all defendants released on various types of bail, approximately 22% fail to appear in court.

Depending on the size of his agency, a bail agent might not be able to spend too much time tracking down a missing defendant. Most bail agencies have only one or two employees. In such cases, the bail agents might spend a week or two on the case or perhaps just make a few phone calls before turning the case over to a BEA.

Bail enforcement agents

Bail enforcement is a specialized field within the private investigation industry. BEAs locate people who don't want to be found.

Being a BEA doesn't require a college education. However, a person can take courses that offer a special certification. In these courses, a person learns practical information, such as how to handcuff a defendant or use pepper spray. Certified BEAs are usually more reliable, and bail agents hire them more consistently.

Few state laws regulate or restrict bail enforcement agents, but in a state like Kentucky, BEAs must notify local authorities before arresting a skip that absconded there. Even then, the authorities may or may not cooperate with the BEA, which means they might inform the BEA that he is working at his own risk and that he could be charged with kidnapping if he arrests anyone within the state. In Nevada, BEAs are strictly regulated. A person must be 21 and a U.S. citizen with a high school diploma. Candidates in Nevada can't have any felony convictions on their record and must pass a drug test and psychiatric exam.

BEAs can carry a badge. However, they are not law enforcement officers and should not be confused with police or any other law enforcement agency.

Television shows and movies portray bounty hunting as dangerous and dramatic. But the first stage in searching for a skip is simply gathering information about the missing person from the papers filed with the bail agent and other court documents, as well as from the person's family and friends. The BEA then evaluates and processes clues that might lead to the defendant in the shortest amount of time with the least amount of danger.

Sometimes the defendant is easy to locate: people who aren't career criminals have no experience in eluding law enforcement. But sometimes the search is longer and more dramatic. In California, BEAs have the right to carry guns, the right to arrest and the right to break down doors while looking for a fugitive or bail jumper. They can also handcuff the defendant and take him to jail. These rights vary from state to state.

BEAs are usually self-employed, although some large bail bond agencies hire bounty hunters full time or part time so they have a reliable source for bail enforcement services. A bail agent hires one BEA for a case, because if two agents are hired for the same case, they might interfere with each other and reduce the chance that the defendant will be found. However, most BEAs end up working as a team.

Finding someone who doesn't want to be found often requires sitting and watching a house where the defendant might be hiding. On television, the fugitive usually leaves the house within a few minutes, and the police or bounty hunters apprehend him. In reality, BEAs might have to watch a place on a stakeout that can last for days. A stakeout of this duration is difficult for one person to handle effectively, so BEAs might team up.

In addition, BEAs maintain a relationship with law enforcement agencies. They will notify the local police department when they are going to pick up a defendant within their jurisdiction and will ask for backup if needed. This is an especially good practice when an agent is in an unfamiliar city looking for a defendant who skipped bail.

Establishing and maintaining a relationship with a good BEA is important for every bail agent. If the bail agent secures the services of a BEA, he provides the BEA with a "right to arrest" form allowing the bounty hunter to arrest the defendant on behalf of the bail agent. Again, the guidelines for BEAs vary from state to state, so check your state's procedures – these can usually be obtained from the state bail association or investigator's association.

When hiring a BEA, bail agents should look for the following qualities:

- Experience: Find someone who has been in business for some time and has references.
- Reliable reputation: A reliable BEA keeps the bail agent updated every few days on the status of the search and doesn't lie about the status. Ask around to find someone with a good reputation.
- Appropriate behavior: The bail agent is liable for the BEA's actions. Find someone who won't put your career in jeopardy. For instance, avoid bounty hunters who make a big show of all their guns or tell tales of how they beat up someone who gave them a hard time.

Often BEAs who don't talk a big talk are the best. Former police officers can make great bounty hunters because they already know the laws well. They also understand the proper way to handle defendants.

Finding a reliable BEA takes some trial and error. The easiest way to find one is to ask your surety company or other bail agents in your area. When you find a BEA, you should ask for references. It might be necessary to hire different BEAs until you find one who is reliable and compatible with your style.

Bounty hunters are often stereotyped as big, aggressive men, but they don't have to be physically large, aggressive or even male. Some of the most effective BEAs are female. They appear less threatening to the defendant. This allows them to get closer to the defendant, which leads to easier identification and capture.

A BEA will refuse to accept a case if he doesn't believe it will pay well enough to cover the time and effort required.

Sometimes a BEA doesn't want to take a case that will require travel, and sometimes he is too busy tracking down other defendants. But the danger of a case rarely deters a BEA. Most consider a dangerous case an interesting challenge.

How long does a bail agent try to find a defendant who has skipped? Sometimes days or weeks pass, and the BEA does not uncover any leads. At this point, the bail agent can either hire another bounty hunter to see if his skills and luck will provide a better result, or the bail agent can trust the judgment of the original BEA and close the case. This means the bail agent will need to begin the process of collecting on the collateral and paying the bail. Of the 22% of defendants that fail to appear in court after being released on bond, approximately one fourth are still fugitives after one year.

If the BEA believes he is close to locating the defendant but needs more time, the bail agent can hire an attorney to file a motion with the courts to extend the time before the full amount of bail is due. The BEA will need to provide a declaration indicating that with a little more time, he believes he can get the defendant back into custody. Judges weigh the facts of each case before deciding whether to give the bail agent more time. If it seems that the BEA has a good lead and isn't wasting the court's time, the judge will probably grant the bail agent an extension.

The laws on extensions vary by state. Some states have a remitter period, which means that once a defendant fails to appear, the bail agent has a certain amount of time to locate him, with no extension. If the defendant is not found within that period of time, the bail agent must pay off the bond. Then he can decide whether or not to continue looking for the defendant. If he finds the defendant, he might receive a portion of the bail amount back from the court. Courts prefer to have defendants appear to answer the charges against them than to have a bail agent pay the bail.

The business details between a bail agent and a BEA are not regulated, but there is a customary way of doing things. For example, it is customary to advance the BEA some cash to pay for gasoline, meals and other incidental expenses. Of course, you should keep a record of these transactions, so you have an accurate record of investigative expenses to charge the cosigner.

When a BEA delivers a defendant to the jail, he gives the bail agent a copy of the booking sheet or a receipt from the jailhouse to prove that the defendant has been delivered. The BEA also submits an invoice and receipts so he can be reimbursed for airfare, hotel rooms and other expenses incurred while tracking down the defendant. All of this is added to the investigative expenses charged to the cosigner.

The costs for locating a defendant who has skipped can mount fairly quickly. Costs include the investigation fees, certified copies of the court docket, background and credit check fees, time spent searching for the defendant, legal motions in the court and possible collections against the cosigner. The fees continue to add up as the investigation continues. This is a reminder of why it is very important to obtain as much information as you can before you post the bond for your defendants.

The bail industry has a maxim that says: Get the money and as much information as possible while the tears are flowing. When a defendant is in jail, he will tell you whatever you need to know. After he is released, it will be much more difficult to get information from him.

As long as the cost of locating the defendant is reasonably less than the bail amount, the bail agent may invest time and money into the search. If the defendant is not found, the cosigner and ultimately the bail agent will be responsible for the costs incurred plus the bail amount. That's why good judgment must be used when choosing to post a bail bond for clients in the first place.

Time's up! A bail agent's liability

The bail agent always faces the possibility that a defendant won't show up for trial and won't be apprehended within the time allotted. The court will issue a "Notice of Full Bail Amount Due." This means the bail agent is liable to the court for the bail amount.

Now what?

This is where the BUF comes in. To prepare for this worst-case scenario, bail agents regularly pay 10% of their income into the BUF account. At this point, the bail agent has a choice: he can pay the court himself or authorize his surety company to access the BUF account to pay the court. If there's not enough money in the BUF account, the surety company will make the payment to the court anyway. The surety company will then reimburse itself when the account has been replenished.

Ultimately the bail agent will be responsible to reimburse the surety company for the bond. There is no time limit to repay the surety but you will want to act as quickly as possible. Otherwise, the surety has the ability to cut you off and not allow you to write bail for them any longer. Then you will need to go to a new surety company and explain why your former surety company cancelled your contract. This process can take weeks or months. Meanwhile, you are still paying all of your advertising and business expenses and not earning any money. It is always wise to stay in good relations with your surety company and conduct your business in a professional manner.

To reimburse the surety company, the bail agent now has to sell the boat or house or whatever collateral he was given so he can replenish his BUF account. The surety company can choose to suspend issuing more bonds to the bail agent until the account has an adequate balance. This process goes more quickly and smoothly if the bail agent had all the appropriate paperwork filled out from the beginning and kept all the documents in the appropriate file. Even so, selling an automobile or piece of real estate can take time.

Most defendants who offer their own property as collateral won't leave their house to be foreclosed on. But if they do skip, the bail agent can foreclose on the house. Realistically, if someone skips bail, they probably are not going to be making their monthly mortgage payments from Mexico or China. So the bank might begin the foreclosure process first.

This is where the lien comes in. The lien tells the bank or anyone else who tries to do something with that piece of property that the bail agent has a stake in it and needs to be paid. The bail agent will eventually be paid from the proceeds of the sale of the house or will have the option of purchasing the home for what the bank is owed. Sometimes the bank is owed much less than the house is worth, so a bail agent can pick up the house for very little money. But this doesn't happen often.

The hassles of a forfeited bond or a skipped defendant will teach new bail agents pretty quickly how important it is to make bail decisions wisely. Even so, the most experienced agents can find themselves on the wrong end of a forfeited bond. Having all the appropriate systems in place – the BUF account, a good bounty hunter, knowledge of the system – helps ensure that the experience will cost less time and money.

8

OTHER TYPES OF BONDS

Though bail bonds are the primary focus of a bail agent's business, he is not limited to transactions concerning bail bonds. A bail agent is the appointed representative of his surety company and may write other types of bonds offered. Those most closely related to the bail agent's main line of work are federal bonds, immigration bonds, child custody bonds, and appeal bonds. Bail agents might also look into offering civil or surety bonds. All of these bonds generate premiums similar to a bail bond and might create extra income when the bail bond business is slow.

Federal bonds

Bail bonds for crimes heard in U.S. district courts are called federal bonds, as U.S. district courts deal with federal offenses such as interstate crime or treason against the United States. Like other bonds, federal bonds release a person from jail on the guarantee he'll appear at all court proceedings, and forfeited bonds are paid to the U.S. government. These bonds are provided by surety companies.

There is no federal bail schedule. At the arraignment, the judge determines the bail amount, which is usually high. Small crimes such as shoplifting or traffic violations aren't heard in federal courts. Only serious crimes that call for serious bail. A bail agent is able to write federal bonds for a premium that can range from 10-15% of the set bail amount.

Federal bonds can provide a significant profit for the bail agent. However, these bonds also carry significant risk. They are large bonds written for people facing very serious charges, which means they are more likely to flee. The cases also last much longer than cases in local or state courts, so the bail agent is exposed to forfeiture longer than for other cases.

Immigration bonds

Immigration bonds are a type of federal bond set for people in custody that are held by the U.S. Immigration & Naturalization Service (INS) pending their court appearance. Immigration bonds are for people who have run into trouble with the Bureau of Immigration and Customs Enforcement (ICE). This is a relatively new government department formed in the federal reorganization after Sept. 11, 2001, to improve homeland security. It includes the INS and Department of Customs. This bond involves aliens – people who are not citizens of the United States.

Aliens require immigration bonds under two circumstances. The first is when a warrant is issued for the alien's arrest for immigration violations, e.g., an individual who has overstayed his visa or green card. In this type of case, ICE requires that the alien appear for a hearing or interview. ICE will issue a "Notice to Obligor to Deliver

Alien" (Form I-340), and the alien then may be eligible for a delivery bond that will allow him to remain free while he awaits his immigration hearing.

The alien must be eligible for bond under the Code of Federal Regulations 8 CFR 236.1, which deals with apprehension, custody and detention of aliens. The alien also must demonstrate to the immigration officer that his release would not pose a danger to property or persons, and that he is likely to appear for all proceedings in his case. The amount of the delivery bond must be sufficient to further ensure that the alien will appear for any future immigration proceedings.

The second circumstance in which an alien might require a bond is when he is permitted to voluntarily leave the United States after removal proceedings have taken place or are scheduled to take place. This is opposed to a forced departure, in which officers physically place the alien on a vessel headed out of the country. Immigration judges may require that someone post a bond in an amount that will ensure that the alien leaves the country within the time specified by the court order.

After ICE determines that an alien is eligible for either a delivery bond ($1,500 minimum) or is granted a voluntary departure with bond ($500 minimum), there are two methods for posting these bonds: cash bond or surety bond.

A cash bond must be paid directly to the ICE and must be posted for the full amount of the bond in one of four forms: cash, money order, cashier's check or U.S. bonds or notes. No form of collateral will be accepted for a cash bond, and a bail agent's service isn't required.

To post a surety bond, the alien must work through a

private bail or surety company, which is usually located in the general vicinity of ICE offices that accept bonds. The requirements for collateral and premiums vary, and ICE does not endorse any one company over another.

The following information is required for posting a bond:

1. Alien Name
2. Alien Registration Number
3. Name of the facility where the alien is being held
4. Alien's home address
5. Alien's date of birth
6. Alien's country of birth
7. Bond amount
8. Name of the person posting the bond
9. Valid address for the person posting the bond
10. Valid Social Security Number for the person posting the bond
11. Valid phone number for the person posting the bond
12. Acceptable form of identification: Permanent resident card, passport with appropriate stamps, valid driver's license, or state identification with proof of immigration status

When immigration bonds are cancelled or discharged because they are no longer needed, the person who posted cash for the bond is notified by ICE that he can file for a refund of the principal plus any accrued interest. If the bonded alien fails to appear when requested by the ICE, the bond is breached, which is another term for forfeited. When cash bonds are breached, ICE is entitled to keep the principal amount. In that case, the obligor (cosigner) is still entitled to receive a payment of accrued interest.

Immigration bonds are very high risk and most surety companies do not write them. Those that do write immigration bonds charge between 15-20%. Collateral is usually required and can range from cash to real property, land, credit cards, bank accounts and CDs. Most surety companies require solid collateral for these bonds and will not allow cars, boats, jewelry, etc. to be used as collateral. The immigration bond can be posted by anyone, including the defendant. Bail agents rarely post immigration bonds, and those that do require a particular license.

Child custody bonds

The child custody bond is quickly gaining acceptance in the bail industry, as a growing number of single parents struggle to protect their children from abduction by the other parent. Each year, over 350,000 children are abducted by a parent or other close family member, usually during a divorce or other custody dispute. The child custody bond helps ensure that parents will abide by the visitation or custody arrangements ordered by the courts, whether the plan involves custody within U.S. borders or internationally.

For more than a decade, the National Center for Missing and Exploited Children (NCMEC) sought to broaden the use of bonds as a tool to prevent parental abductions or assist the parents left behind. NCMEC formed a partnership with the

Professional Bail Agents of the United States to create the child custody bond, which is now licensed in 38 states and being considered in more. PBUS provides informational programs nationwide to educate its agents and surety companies about the child custody bond. These bonds were designed to assist the searching parent with financial resources. If a parent buys a child custody bond and absconds with the child, the other parent will be paid the amount of the bond which will allow that parent to search for the child.

The child custody bond works as follows: If one parent hasn't been complying with the custody terms or has given the other parent suspicion that he will stop following the custody and visitation terms, the suspicious parent can request that a child custody bond be ordered by the court. The judge will hear the case, determine if the bond is needed and, if so, will set the amount.

The bond amount should be large enough to not only discourage abduction and help ensure compliance with custody arrangements, but also provide a sum large enough to finance a search for the child in case of an abduction. Parents who abduct their children generally have nothing to lose financially by breaking the court-ordered custody agreement, yet the parents left behind can be faced with staggering bills for lawyers and private investigators in trying to get their children back. Usually child custody bonds are set between \$10,000 and \$50,000, with international bonds set at higher levels such as \$100,000.

As with other bonds, collateral is needed. Grandparents, employers or friends can provide the necessary collateral, which can be cash, real estate or other items standard for collateral. A judge can order both parents to post such a bond. The bond can be used to protect both parents, including the one who doesn't have custody. For example, if a parent refuses to allow visitation as ordered by the court, the bond can be put into play. The parent who has been wrongfully denied visitation can have the bond forfeited and use the money to wage a legal battle to enforce the visitation rights outlined in the custody agreement.

Bail agents are already familiar with the basic concept behind a child custody bond, because it mirrors a bail bond: A bond is issued to provide incentive for a person to do something, e.g., to appear in court or abide by a child custody agreement. Collateral is taken to secure the amount of the bond. Should the person under bond fail to do what he is supposed to do, the bond is forfeited. However, instead of the bond money going to the court as in a bail case, the proceeds of the child custody bond go to the other parent to provide the resources to find the child or children.

In response to the rise in international child abduction, the United States has taken several steps. First, it is a signatory to the Hague Convention on the Civil Aspects of International Child Abduction. The introduction states that "The States signatory to the present Convention, Firmly convinced that the interests of children are of paramount importance in matters relating to their custody, Desiring to protect children internationally from the harmful effects of their wrongful removal or retention and to establish procedures to ensure their prompt return to the State of their habitual residence, as well as to secure protection for rights of access, Have resolved to conclude a Convention to this effect."

The convention outlines provisions about returning children to the custodial parents, whether through judicial proceedings or other means. The problem is that not all nations have signed on to the convention. Therefore, a parent who takes a child into a non-signing country leaves the remaining parent with a monumental legal battle. That's where a child custody bond might come in handy. In cases where an international abduction is feared, the bond amount is set high enough to cover the increased legal and investigative expenses of an international search.

A second measure to thwart international child abduction occurred when Congress amended passport procedures for children younger than 14 years of age. The requirement, effective July 2001, requires the consent of both parents before a U.S. passport can be issued to a child younger than 14. In addition, the U.S. Department of State's Passport Issuance Alert Program is still available to parents involved in a custody dispute or concerned about the possibility of an international child abduction. After a child's name is entered into the alert system, the parent is notified if a passport is ordered for the child.

Of course, loopholes exist. A child might already have a passport, making it easier for a parent to sneak the child out of the country undetected. Therefore, child abductions still occur despite these measures, and a bail agent can do his part in preventing the abductions by learning how to implement a child custody bond.

Appeal bonds

When a person is found guilty of a crime, he will sometimes appeal the sentence in an effort to get a new trial or a better verdict. On the day the person was sentenced, the original bail bond was exonerated. This means that if the defendant wants to stay out of jail while awaiting the appeal, he needs to post an appeal bond.

The amount of the bond is usually higher than for ordinary bail bonds, because the defendant has been found guilty and most likely faces jail time. The bail agent receives his usual premium on an appeal bond, but many agents also require cash collateral because of the high risk. Many agents avoid these bonds altogether because of the increased risk.

Civil and surety bonds

A surety bond is a general bond by which one party makes itself responsible for a certain debt or obligation. In other words, the cosigner guarantees through collateral that a financial obligation will be met or a service will be performed. These are civil bonds that ensure the performer will do his job properly and if anything goes wrong, the surety will back it up. One such bond is a contract bond, which protects the recipient against loss in case the terms of a contract are not filled. The surety company assumes liability for nonperformance of the items outlined in the contract, whether it's delivery of a product or service. Surety bonds are also involved in the state licensing requirements for contractors, notaries, auto dealers and other professionals.

For example, if you hire a contractor to do a large job, such as constructing an office building to house your new bail bond business, you can take out a performance bond, which guarantees the job will be finished properly. If the contractor forfeits the bond, i.e., doesn't finish the project, the collateral on the bond is used to pay another contractor to complete the project. Therefore, you are assured of getting your new bail bond office. Another type of bond, the payment bond, works similarly. It guarantees that the work will be completed without liens for the cost of labor or materials being taken out on the property.

Most contractors have contractor license bonds required by the state as part of licensing procedures, but those don't necessarily protect a homeowner whose contractor never finished that new roof. They enable the state to collect fines for violations the contractor has committed or to protect against work that violates building codes. These bonds rarely cover actual reimbursement of claims by homeowners. So business owners or homeowners investing a large sum of money into a building or remodeling project might be looking for someone to post a surety bond to protect their investment.

Bail agents can find out from their surety company which bonds the surety offers and what the terms and premiums are on each. As mentioned before, bail agents can sign up with more than one surety company if one offers a product that another doesn't.

9

LEGAL SYSTEM 101

The judicial system plays a key role in the bail industry. The courts determine whether bail is appropriate or available to the defendant. Judges set the bail schedules. Because the bail agent is a key part of the criminal justice system, it will help if you understand the structure of the system and the processes involved with allowing a person his day in court.

Court system basics

The American judicial system ranges from local magistrates who resolve disputes between neighbors to the U.S. Supreme Court, which resolves disputes in interpretations of laws, especially as they relate to the U.S. Constitution.

States, cities and counties are divided into jurisdictions, which refers to the area over which a certain court has power. For example, if someone is arrested in Pasadena, that person is in the jurisdiction of the Los Angeles County courts. Most suspects will have their cases heard at the courthouse in the jurisdiction where they were arrested. Typically the jail is near the courthouse for that jurisdiction. However, if a person is murdered in one county by a defendant from another county, the case could be filed in either county.

Jurisdiction sometimes refers to the subject of a case, not the geography. For example, a bankruptcy court is one that has jurisdiction over bankruptcy cases but would not be able to settle a dispute over a traffic court violation. It would not have the jurisdiction to do so. Courts may be limited in their jurisdiction. For example, small claims courts typically can't handle claims involving more than $5,000 in damages.

Another word relating to the location of a trial is "venue." This means the physical, geographical location where the defendant will be standing when he is on trial. The venue of a court case is not always within the physical location of the jurisdiction. An attorney on either side can file a motion for a change of venue. This means the attorney believes the trial would be fairer if it were held somewhere else. For example, lawyers for Scott Peterson, accused of killing his pregnant wife Laci Peterson, asked for a change of venue because they felt they could not find an unbiased jury in the couple's hometown of Modesto, where media coverage of the case was relentless. A change of venue was granted, and the trial was moved 90 miles away to San Mateo County.

Changing the venue does not mean changing the legal jurisdiction. The same judges and the same district attorney from the court in which the case was filed will still be the judges and attorneys in the case following the change of venue. They will simply have to drive farther and go to trial in an unfamiliar courthouse.

Two types of cases are heard in courtrooms: civil cases

and criminal cases. Civil cases involve disputes between people or companies, e.g., one person suing another for breach of contract, or an employee suing a company because of a personal injury. A divorce is a civil case. The government can also bring civil cases against individuals or companies.

Criminal cases are brought between the government and a person accused of breaking the government's laws, meaning a crime has been committed.

The structure of U.S. courts

The U.S. government has three branches: executive (the president and his executive agencies), legislative (Congress and related lawmaking bodies), and judicial (the courts that interpret and apply the laws). Federal courts are divided into three levels. State courts are divided into three or four levels, depending on the state.

Most state constitutions outline the judicial system for that state. The system varies from one state to the next, and sometimes the same label will have a different definition depending on the state. For example, the terms "circuit" and "district" are used at the state and federal levels, but they don't always have the same meaning from one state to the next. A good primer for all the state systems can be found at the National Center for State Courts website (http://www.ncsconline.org), which provides links to each state's judicial web pages (click on "Links" to find the link to individual court websites). Or visit your state's official website and follow the relevant links.

Despite their differences, each state's court system has a

similar layout. The lowest level of courts in each state usually consists of local courts. These might be called local justice courts, district justice courts, municipal courts or magistrate courts. These courts hear the lowest level of judicial cases, e.g., violations of city and borough ordinances, simple domestic violence cases or other misdemeanors. Some of these lower-level courts have special topic jurisdictions, such as juvenile court, small-claims court or traffic court.

Some states have county courts, while others have a system of district courts that hear the next level of cases. Others have a court of common pleas at this level, while still others have circuit courts. Whatever the state calls it, this next level of courts is the first level where "real" cases are heard: felonies, cases involving larger financial claims than can be handled in small claims court, family court matters, etc. Some misdemeanors might be heard at this level, depending on how the state's lower courts are set up.

The next level up is usually the appellate court. Cases generally do not originate in this court. The appellate court reviews cases that have already been decided by a lower court when one of the parties has appealed the lower court's decision. In some states, the appellate court is called the court of appeals. Some states might use the term superior court for an appellate court, as opposed to calling the lower district court a superior court. Some states divide the appellate court into two courts based on topic jurisdiction: civil or criminal. Again, each state is different in terms of specifics, and you will need to take some time to learn the structure for your state.

Regardless of the names and divisions for the lower

courts, every state has at the head of its judicial system a state supreme court. This is the highest judicial authority in each state. The state supreme court reviews cases appealed from the appellate court system. If a party still is not satisfied with the verdict after the case is reviewed by the state supreme court, he can appeal to the U.S. Supreme Court.

Beyond the state court structure are the federal courts. These are reserved for certain cases when:

- Federal laws have been violated.
- Constitutional issues are involved.
- The dispute involves two states or residents of different states.
- The United States is a party in the dispute.

The lowest federal court is the district court. The entire country is divided into districts. Large states like California are their own district. If someone doesn't like a ruling in the district court, he can appeal to the federal court of appeals.

The federal court of appeals has jurisdiction in areas called circuits. These circuits cover several districts, so even a large state like California shares the circuit court with its neighbors, e.g., Oregon, Nevada and several other states and territories.

If a party is not satisfied with the ruling given at the federal circuit court level, he can appeal to the top of the federal judicial structure: the U.S. Supreme Court. The Supreme Court, an appellate court, reviews the facts of the case and decides whether to hear it. The Supreme Court hears very few of the cases presented to it. It lets most cases stand, which means the decision of the lower court is the final verdict. Once a case has reached the Supreme Court, the appellate process is over. There is no higher court to which a party can appeal, and the party must accept the outcome.

Courtrooms: A guided tour

Now that you understand how the judicial system works, let's look at the inner workings of the courtroom. The players within the courtroom include the judge, a public defender or defense attorney, one or more deputy district attorneys, one or two bailiffs, a transcriber and one or two court clerks. There's also the defendant – the person defending himself against the charges. Although as a bail agent you might not appear in a courtroom every day, it helps to have an understanding of who these players are.

Judges

Judges are in charge of everything that goes on in the courtroom. Federal judges and many state judges are appointed. The president of the United States or the state governor nominates judges, who then must be confirmed by Congress or the state's legislature. Some states elect judges for a specified term, after which they must campaign for reelection. Judges hearing criminal cases specialize in criminal law.

District attorney

As the name implies, the district attorney is the attorney for a district or jurisdiction. The district attorney prosecutes defendants on behalf of the people of the county or state. For most citizens, the district attorney is the "good guy," as he is protecting citizens by enforcing the law. For a defendant, the district attorney is the "bad guy," because he is trying to put the defendant in jail.

In California, each county has a head district attorney and several deputy district attorneys. Deputy district attorneys are assigned to individual courtrooms on a case-by-case basis. District attorneys and deputy district attorneys are involved only in criminal cases – you won't find them in the traffic court, for example.

Defense attorney

The defense attorney is the lawyer hired by the defendant to represent him in court. The defense attorney's goal is to have the case dismissed or the defendant proven innocent or the minimum punishment imposed for the crime if the defendant is found guilty.

Bailiff

The bailiff is usually a deputy sheriff for the county. The bailiff calls the court to order, usually saying, "All rise, 'X' Court is now in session. The Honorable John Q. Smith presiding. You may be seated." The bailiff's duties are far from ceremonial. He maintains order in the courtroom and handles the flow of cases and people. He calls and swears in witnesses, seats juries and can also arrest individuals if the judge so orders. If a verdict is read and the defendant is found guilty, the bailiff will handcuff the defendant and escort him from the courtroom.

Transcriber or court reporter

To create a transcript, all courts have some means of recording every court proceeding, either by making an electronic audio recording or by having a court reporter create a typed transcript. Most court reporters are outside contractors, not employees of the court. Although it may look like the transcriber is typing in the old-fashioned way, some modern court transcription machines are hooked up to computers that transform the transcript instantly into digital files that can be accessed in the courtroom in real time.

Court clerk

The court clerk is the person that you, as a bail agent, will work with most often. Some courts even have a bond clerk responsible for handling all the court's bail bonds. Most communication with the clerks is done by telephone, but the bail agent may visit the bond clerk at the courthouse to obtain proof of exoneration or any other documents related to a bail bond.

Some courts have a computer database that can create bond reports showing all of the bonds a bail agency has written in that specific court, or in the entire county. The report lists the status of the cases, next court dates, exonerations, forfeitures and anything the court has done regarding the case. A bail agent might call the clerk to request a copy of this valuable report and then stop to pick it up at the courthouse. But at most courthouses, bail agents have to ask for the status of their bonds case by case.

Public defender

If a defendant can't afford a lawyer, the court will appoint a public defender, who is an attorney licensed by the state to represent such defendants, to allow them the fair trial to which they are entitled.

Physical courtroom setting

The physical arrangement of courtrooms is similar across the country. If a defendant is present for a bail hearing, he will be seated in the custody "box" at the front of the courtroom. All those in custody usually enter the courtroom through a special front entrance and remain in the box during their hearing. Many courts handcuff the defendants to each other until all of their cases have been heard, and then each defendant is escorted by an officer back to the jail or holding facility in the court. If a defendant is coming into his trial or hearing and was not able – or not permitted – to post bail, he will still be in jail up to the trial date and will be brought to the court by the sheriff's department. Defendants who are out on bail will be free to walk into court on their own or with their attorney.

Of course, the judge gets the best seat, usually elevated, front and center in the courtroom. During a trial, the rows of seats in the box to one side of the judge's bench will be filled with the jury. The table to the judge's right as he looks out over the courtroom will be for the defendant and his attorney. The prosecutor and any assistants will be on his left.

Different court proceedings have different terms. An arraignment is the court appearance in which the defendant enters a plea of guilty or not guilty. The arraignment is not a trial, only a hearing. There are no witnesses or testimony. It is usually a discussion between attorneys and the judge. This occurs early in the process, usually within days after the defendant is arrested.

At the arraignment, if the defendant does not have an attorney, the judge will tell him he is entitled to an attorney and that a public defender will be appointed for him if he can't afford an attorney. If the defendant pleads guilty, the judge will read the maximum sentencing for that crime to be sure the defendant knows what he is pleading guilty to. If a "not guilty" plea is entered, the discussion might turn to bail.

If the defendant does not have a bail amount set or his bail is too high, his attorney will ask the judge to set a bail amount or reduce the bail. In most cases the bail amount will already be set. Some cases are too serious, however, for the arresting agencies to set bail, so they will wait for the judge to set the bail.

If the charges are more serious, a bail hearing may be scheduled for later to allow time to address the matter properly. Defense attorneys will always make a plea that bail be set. However, if the crime is extremely serious, or the defendant has violated probation in the past, bail is usually not allowed. Sometimes the defendant has a parole hold. This means he has served time in jail for a previous crime and committed the new crime while on parole. He cannot be issued bail until the hold is lifted or a judge approves.

Defendants have a constitutional right to a speedy trial. In California, the arraignment usually takes placed within 72 hours of the arrest. However, depending on whether weekends or holidays are involved, it could be up to five days before a defendant may appear before a judge. After the arraignment, the defendant's attorney may waive the right to a speedy trial to have more time to prepare his case.

Once the arraignment is over and bail has been set or denied, the next court date is the preliminary hearing. In the preliminary hearing, evidence is heard to allow the judge to determine whether there is enough of a case to warrant a trial. If a trial is warranted, the judge will set the trial date. If not, the case will be dismissed, the defendant released and the bail bond exonerated.

When the bail agent issues a bond for the release of the defendant, the defendant stays out of jail until the case is over and a sentence is pronounced, even if the case goes on for a long time. Only if the defendant misses a court appearance or commits a new crime, or if new facts are discovered that would cause the bail agent or court to revoke bail, would the defendant be required to return to jail.

Most felony cases don't make it to trial – only three percent are settled by juries. Most are resolved with a guilty plea. The others are dismissed for lack of evidence or other legal issues.

As a bail agent, you will not typically be involved in defendants' cases once they have been released from custody, unless a judge raises the defendant's bail and requires an additional bond. You might also go to court to surrender a defendant back to custody. This would happen if the defendant either missed a court date or did not meet all the requirements of the bail agreement and you had to track him down.

If you do need to appear in court, you need to follow some basic guidelines:

- Wear a suit and tie.
- If you're wearing a hat, remove it when you enter the courtroom.
- Always address the judge as "Your Honor."
- Never talk unless addressed during a hearing or trial.
- If the judge addresses you, stand up while you speak to him, then sit back down as soon as the exchange is finished.
- Stand when the judge enters or leaves the courtroom.
- Turn off your cell phone or pager or put them on "vibrate."
- Do not smoke or bring food or drink into a courtroom.

Language of lawyers: A vocabulary lesson

It's helpful for bail agents to become familiar with some of the courthouse jargon, so they can follow along with the conversations of court officials or law enforcement officers. Here are some of the terms you will hear most frequently:

Acquit – what the jury does when it finds a defendant not guilty; e.g., *He was acquitted of the murder charges because the evidence was not very strong.*

Alias – another name that a person uses, often to escape notice from law enforcement. In legal documents, a defendant will be identified by his real name, followed by AKA ("Also Known As") and his list of aliases used to commit crimes.

Appellate court – a court that hears appeals, i.e., a court that considers the same case already heard by another court to ensure the initial court did not violate the law, legal procedures or the defendant's rights; e.g., *The defendant believed his guilty verdict would be thrown out in appellate court because important evidence was wrongfully kept out of his first trial.*

Conviction – when a person is found guilty of a crime through a trial or other judicial process; e.g., *He was convicted of murder because the crime was caught on videotape.*

Capital offense, capital case – referring to cases or offenses where the defendant faces capital punishment, i.e., the death penalty. Murder and treason are capital offenses.

Code – a law or series of laws; e.g., *California Penal Code.*

Disposition – the finishing or "disposing" of a case, the final outcome, usually a sentence for the defendant. Not to be confused with **deposition**, a statement a witness makes under oath before a trial begins.

Docket – a calendar of cases waiting to be heard in a court. A docket sheet shows all of the defendant's court appearances for a certain case and any orders or rulings coming out of each appearance; e.g., *The Jones case is on the docket for next week, but I think he skipped town.*

Extradition – refers to situations in which a person who has been accused or convicted of a crime in one jurisdiction, such as a particular state, is arrested in another jurisdiction and needs to be handed back to the first jurisdiction for trial or to finish his jail sentence.

Felony – a serious crime punishable by at least one year or more in prison, up to and including the death penalty. Assault with a deadly weapon, for example, is a felony.

Fugitive from justice – a person who commits a crime and then either hides in the state where the crime was committed or flees to another state to avoid being put on trial and possibly convicted.

Grand jury – a group of people who hear evidence against a person accused of a crime to decide whether there are grounds to file charges against that person. The grand jury does not decide a person's innocence or guilt, only whether the prosecutors have enough evidence to go to trial. A trial jury determines innocence or guilt.

Hearing – a court proceeding in which certain facts in a case are decided or issues resolved, usually open to the public; e.g., *The defendant was denied bail at his bail hearing after evidence was presented that he was a flight risk.*

Hung jury – when the 12 members of a jury are unable to agree whether a person is innocent or guilty.

Incarcerate – to confine someone to jail or prison; e.g., *He was incarcerated without bail while he awaited his trial on charges of armed robbery.*

Indictment – a written statement from a grand jury that formally charges a person with a crime, thus moving the case forward to the courts for trial; e.g., *The grand jury indicted Michael Jackson on sexual assault charges, so the case went to trial.*

In custody – when a person is under the control of law enforcement officers, usually in a jail, prison or other detention center.

Infraction – a minor crime such as a traffic violation for which a person can be fined but not sent to jail.

Misdemeanor – a minor crime punishable by a fine or confinement in a jail or detention center other than a prison. Shoplifting a small item, for example, is a misdemeanor.

Mistrial – a trial that is ended without a verdict. A mistrial can result from a hung jury, the death of a key player such as an attorney or juror, or by some event in the proceedings that makes it impossible for the defendant to receive a fair verdict.

Motion – a procedure that lawyers or defendants must follow when they want the judge to make an official court order; e.g., *The defense attorney filed a motion for the case to be continued to a later date so he could have more time to prepare.*

Nol pros – courtroom jargon for a case that's been dismissed. Short for *nolle prosequi*: "unwilling to prosecute."

Nolo contendere – when a defendant pleads "no contest," which means he is not pleading guilty or not guilty but is willing to accept the consequences of a guilty verdict.

Prosecutor – the attorney bringing the charges against the defendant and trying to prove the case against the defendant.

Statute – another word for a law.

Statute of limitations – the time limit set by law for a specific legal action to occur. For example, a person can't be arrested for a crime if the statute of limitations says the person must be tried within five years and six years have passed. An individual can't sue for damages in certain situations after a specified length of time has passed.

Suspended sentence – a sentence that the defendant doesn't actually have to serve if he plays his cards right. For example, if he receives a three-month suspended sentence, he does not go to jail unless he violates the terms of the suspension, which usually specify that he can't be arrested for another crime within a certain time period.

Verdict – the decision by the jury as to whether the defendant is guilty or not guilty.

Warrant – an authorization by a judge for an officer to search a location, seize items or arrest a suspect.

Writ – an order written on behalf of a court or other person in the legal system that compels the person named in the writ to comply with whatever orders are outlined in the writ. For example, a court issues a writ of execution to a sheriff or other officer to carry out a judgment on behalf of the individual who won the right to obtain a certain property in court, so the sheriff can go and seize that property and hand it over to the individual who won the judgment.

10

TALES FROM A BAIL AGENT

I've been working as a bail agent in California for 12 years. In those years, I've posted close to 5,000 bonds for defendants, with charges ranging from unpaid civil fines to vehicular manslaughter charges. Drugs, DUI's, driving with suspended licenses, domestic violence, assault and battery, evading police, public drunkenness, fighting, insurance fraud, credit card and identity theft, writing bad checks, weapons charges – you name it, my agency has bailed them out.

We have bailed out different types of individuals: engineers, writers, doctors, lawyers, plumbers, contractors, salesmen, actors, musicians, real estate agents, loan brokers… just about everyone. Some of the cases go well, some go poorly. For the most part, people pay their fees and show up for court when they're supposed to. But there's always a chance that any case will go in the wrong direction. Here are some real-life cases to better illustrate how the system works.

CASE #1 – Easy money

One man was issued a ticket for not having his dog on a leash as they walked along the beach. He didn't think it was a big deal, so he misplaced the ticket and never paid the fine. The police issued a warrant, arrested the man and put him in jail, with bail set at $500.

The defendant called me. The decision to take the case was a no-brainer. He had lived and worked in the same place his entire life. The bail amount was small. The crime was minimal. And he was in the jail closest to my home. I went to the jail, bailed him out without even requiring collateral, and earned a $50 premium and a $15 administrative fee for virtually no risk. No one could believe the police arrested him for an unpaid dog leash ticket. But because they did, my services were needed.

CASE #2 – All's well that ends well

A father called to post bail for his 19-year-old son who was charged with shooting cars and people with a paintball gun. He was being held on a $100,000 bond. After performing the basic risk assessment, I took the case and posted the bond.

After the second court date, the judge determined that the defendant needed a higher bail to match that of his co-defendants: $150,000. The father called me back. We posted a bond for the additional $50,000. As collateral for the bonds, the father used two properties that had more than $400,000 in equity.

After a year or so of court cases, the defendant's case was resolved and he was sentenced to 18 months in jail and three years probation. When my agency received proof of exoneration of the bond from the court, we re-conveyed the property back to the father.

Most cases that involve real estate go smoothly. As a bail agent, I can say that nothing feels better than to write a good solid bond with a full premium and property as collateral. You post the bond, earn your money, file a lien on the property and wait. Two months later, you get a call saying the defendant has met his obligations to the court and the bond is exonerated. You call the court, obtain the exoneration and remove the lien from the house. It's a good feeling when people meet their obligations and do what they are supposed to do.

CASE #3 – Collateral cars

I received a call from the local jail from a women charged with prostitution for the fifth or sixth time. Over the years, I have learned that individuals charged with prostitution are usually looking at a mandatory 30 to 90 days in jail and that they rarely appear in court because they have drug problems and can't last 30 to 90 days without feeding their drug habit. So it's a basic rule that when bailing a prostitute, you should be sure you have full collateral. In this case, even the woman's parents weren't willing to cosign the bail bond. It was a high-risk case.

Her bail was $5,000. I explained to her over the phone that I required collateral worth more than the $5,000. She said she had a Pontiac Grand Am, approximately two years old. After doing some investigation, I determined her car was worth $8,000 to $9,000. In some cases, I might just ask for the pink slip or even transfer the title while the case is going on, but in this case I thought the defendant would probably not show up in court. I wanted the actual car in my possession.

Her parents were willing to deliver the car and $500 for my fee. They met me at the jail, paid me, gave me the title and the keys to the car and we posted the bond. The woman was released. I had her sign all of the paperwork, including the title to her car. I allowed her to take her personal items out of the car, and then she and her parents went on their way. I had brought my wife with me to drive home one of the cars, so she drove the defendant's car, which of course had no gas.

We stopped at a nearby gas station. When I walked up to the car, my wife had a disgusted and frightened look on her face. As I opened the car door, the handle on the inside fell off and out fell hypodermic needles and drug paraphernalia. To this day, my wife won't drive any collateral cars. The moral of the story is to inspect fully and document in detail the condition of the car and everything in the car prior to leaving with the vehicle. Had the police pulled us over, they very easily could have thought the drugs and paraphernalia were ours.

I drove the car home from the gas station. It sat in our garage for four months until the defendant's case was over. I was sure I was going to have to sell the car to pay off her bond, but she completed all of her court requirements, and everything worked out the way it was supposed to. I returned the car to her, and the case was closed.

CASE #4 – A bail agent's nightmare

A woman from Los Angeles was charged with six counts of child abuse. She was arrested and jailed, with bail set at $100,000. Her parents called my agency. Because it was a large bond, we completed a thorough risk assessment, i.e., we ran a credit check, verified phone numbers of family members, even verified that the defendant went to the college she said she went to. Everything checked out.

As collateral, the parents offered their house, which had over $130,000 in equity. We checked out the property and determined that the parents did have the title and the property did have the equity, so we posted the bond. We earned a $10,000 full premium up front. Nearly an ideal situation for a bail agent… or so I thought.

All of the paperwork was signed and filed. Three days after posting the bond, we went to the county recorder's office to record a lien against the property, just in case something went wrong. Six months passed. Then we received a forfeiture notice from the court. We called the court to see if the notice was a mistake or if the defendant had shown up in the days since the notice was filed.

We called the parents and asked what had happened to their daughter. They said, "We don't know. She disappeared in the middle of the night."

We hired investigators and bounty hunters and also did a lot of work ourselves to track her down. Once the forfeited bond of $100,000 became due to the court, we investigated the property, thinking that we at least had the house for collateral. After doing the title report, we discovered that the house had new liens that were filed just before ours was filed.

The liens were filed by places like The Cash Doctor and Cash-R-Us.

It turned out the clients went to three different loan agents to set up loans right after they posted bail for their daughter. Through the cash loan offices, they had pulled out almost all of the equity in the house. There was not enough equity left for us to proceed with any action on the property. My surety company used the funds from my BUF account to pay the bond. That was money I had earned and built up over the years.

In this case, we were completely set up and taken advantage of by the clients. Two years later, we went to court and won a judgment for $127,000 against the parents. But winning a judgment doesn't mean you get the money. After doing asset searches and credit checks, we found out the parents owned nothing. We couldn't garnish their wages because they had jobs where they received cash under the table. They had no bank accounts or anything in their name.

The defendant has not surfaced to face trial for the charges, and I've never received any money back. This was a good situation gone completely bad.

There's not much you can do when people deliberately set out to cheat you, but you can still take precautionary measures. On large bonds, it's crucial for you to do title searches, background checks, credit checks, etc. Also do a little investigation after the bond is posted to be sure the client is on the up and up. Don't cut any corners when dealing with a large bond. It's too risky.

In this case, the reason the loans didn't come up in our research was because the liens were filed after we completed all of our property checks, but before we filed the deed against the house. We posted bail for the client at night, and a few days later we filed our lien. In those few days, the liens were placed against the house, prior to our lien being filed.

CASE #5 – Small bonds, large debts

Small bonds – those for $1,000 or less – are common for bail agents. Even though the amount is small, it is often wise to require some type of collateral. You might think that because the bail amount is low, the crime was not serious and the defendant won't skip town. But here's how the situation can go wrong.

I posted a $500 bond without collateral. It seemed too much of a hassle to do the extra paperwork on such a small bond. I earned a quick $50. The defendant failed to appear in court. I was faced with paying $500. So I called the cosigner and defendant. Their phones were disconnected. I called all the other phone numbers on the bail bond application and couldn't reach anyone.

This is a situation in which many agents find themselves. They have now spent several dollars on calls and an hour of their time trying to locate the defendant. There's a tough decision to be made: How much time and money do you spend continuing to look for the person?

If you run a background check, you spend another $25 on the case. You earned only $50 to start and paid your bond cost and paid into your BUF account. At this point you have earned very little money. You can't hire a bounty hunter – no bounty hunter will go after a person with a $500 bond. Bounty hunters are paid by percentage, and they would lose money on such a small case.

It's important to be certain who you are bailing out, and protect yourself even if it's a small bond. In this case, it would cost more to locate the defendant than to pay off the bond. The lesson is to secure some type of collateral even when posting small bonds such as this one.

CASE #6 – The dangers of cash

Although it's not common for people to pay cash for bail, I am always on alert when it happens. If it's $100 or $200 in bail fees handed over in a police station at noon, that's not much of a problem, but when it's $1,000 or $2,000 handed over in the middle of the night in a strange neighborhood, it's a little nerve-racking. I want to get the cash to the bank as fast as possible.

I have had several cases where cosigners and others have walked me to my car in the middle of the night after I accepted cash for a bond, because I didn't look like I belonged in their neighborhood. For the most part, the people we deal with are on our side, because we are on their side. We are doing our clients a service and a favor, and they are doing us a favor by using our services.

CASE #7: Sneaking up on a skip

If you have never tracked anyone before, it is likely that you will alert the person you are looking for before you find him. It's critical to learn how to sneak up on someone without them knowing you are even looking for them.

One time I posted bail for a man who was arrested for outstanding traffic tickets. He didn't appear in court when he was supposed to. No one answered the phone at the home where he lived with his girlfriend, so my employee and I drove 200 miles to the town where he lived. We showed up at the restaurant where his girlfriend worked, but she was off that night. Because we were hungry after the long drive, we decided to eat there anyway. After we finished eating, we had some chicken wings left over, so we put them in a carryout box and drove to the defendant's house.

We stood outside the house and heard the girlfriend and a male inside the house talking as they watched television. We assumed the male voice belonged to the defendant, but we couldn't see him. So my employee decided to get the box of leftover chicken wings and pretend he was a delivery person.

He knocked on the door, and the girlfriend asked who was there. My employee said he was from the restaurant and that he had their order. They argued that they didn't order anything. So my employee finally said, "Well, there must be a mistake, so if you want the food, you can have it free."

They opened the door. Sure enough, our defendant was sitting on the floor watching television, thinking he was going to get a free meal.

Capturing a defendant isn't always this easy. I recommend hiring an experienced investigator who has been doing it for a while. Research and interview investigators closely. Anyone with a gun and a fake badge can call themselves an investigator or bounty hunter. Remember that as a bail agent, you are responsible for the investigator's actions. If he hurts the defendant, the odds are you will be sued and found liable for the damages incurred.

A final word

Although there are some negative aspects to being a bail agent, there's a rewarding side as well. It's satisfying to know that people really appreciate our services. Several times I have received compliments, referrals and recommendations from satisfied and even overjoyed clients. Some clients are so scared when they get out of jail they are happy to see a smiling face. I always remember why I do the job when a client gets out of jail and starts crying to me or to his family or friends.

Many times we see people at their lowest moment, when they have hit rock bottom. It's a turning point in their lives. Many of the people for whom we post bail will never go back to jail or be in any trouble again. Most realize they made a mistake and need help. Their cosigners are willing to give their troubled friend or family member one last chance. They post bail for the defendant, and the defendant knows it's do-or-die time.

This job is rewarding because we are helping people at a desperate time of need. In general, people appreciate that. And that's what makes a career as a bail agent worthwhile.

APPENDIX
Resources

To learn more about bail agents, the American criminal justice system, laws of the land and the rights of prisoners, look at the following resources:

Websites

American Bail Coalition
http://www.americanbailcoalition.com/new_html/state_laws_htm

This website highlights laws pertaining to the bail bond industry in each state, including licensing fees and exam requirements.

Professional Bail Agents of the United States
http://www.pbus.com

This website describes the upcoming events and activities of this national bail association, as well as membership and networking opportunities and the latest news affecting the bail industry.

Official state websites

To learn more about licensing requirements for bail agents in a particular state, visit the official website for the regulatory department in that state. Because each state's DOI or Department of Commerce handles many different topics, it's often difficult to find bail agent licensing information quickly. It is sometimes included with licensing information for other types of insurance agents, but even that can be hard to find. If your state's website has the bail agent information buried deep within, try the site's search function. Type in "bail bond" or "surety agent" or "bail bond license" to locate the appropriate section.

If all else fails, each site has a phone number or e-mail address for you to use to obtain more information.

Following is a list of relevant state websites:

Alabama http://www.aldoi.org
Alaska
http://www.dced.state.ak.us/insurance/
Arizona http://www.id.state.az.us
Arkansas
http://www.arkansas.gov/insurance/
California http://www.insurance.ca.gov
Colorado
http://www.dora.state.co.us/insurance
Connecticut http://www.ct.gov/cid
Delaware http://www.state.de.us/inscom
District of Columbia
http://www.disr.washingtondc.gov
Florida http://www.fldfs.com
Georgia http://www.inscomm.state.ga.us
Hawaii http://www.hawaii.gov/dcca/ins
Idaho http://www.doi.state.id.us

Illinois	http://www.ins.state.il.us
Indiana	http://www.in.gov/idoi
Iowa	http://www.iid.state.ia.us/
Kansas	http://www.ksinsurance.org
Kentucky	http://doi.ppr.ky.gov/kentucky/
Louisiana	http://www.ldi.la.gov
Michigan	http://www.michigan.gov/cis
Mississippi	http://www.doi.state.ms.us
Maine	http://www.state.me.us/pfr/ins/ins_index.htm
Maryland	http://www.mdinsurance.state.md.us
Massachusetts	http://www.state.ma.us/doi/
Minnesota	http://www.commerce.state.mn.us
Missouri	http://www.insurance.state.mo.us/
Montana	http://www.sao.state.mt.us
Nebraska	http://www.nol.org/home/NDOI/
Nevada	http://www.doi.state.nv.us
New Hampshire	http://www.nh.gov/insurance
New Jersey	http://www.state.nj.us/dobi
New Mexico	http://www.nmprc.state.nm.us/insurance/inshm.htm
New York	http://www.ins.state.ny.us
North Carolina	http://www.ncdoi.com
North Dakota	http://www.state.nd.us/ndins
Ohio	http://www.ohioinsurance.gov
Oklahoma	http://www.oid.state.ok.us
Oregon	http://www.cbs.state.or.us/external/ins

Pennsylvania http://www.ins.state.pa.us
Rhode Island http://www.dbr.state.ri.us/
South Dakota
http://www.state.sd.us/drr2/reg/insurance/
South Carolina http://www.doi.state.sc.us
Tennessee
http://www.state.tn.us/commerce/
Texas http://www.tdi.state.tx.us
Utah http://www.insurance.utah.gov
Vermont http://www.bishca.state.vt.us
Virginia
http://www.state.va.us/scc/division/boi/
Washington
http://www.insurance.wa.gov
West Virginia http://www.state.wv.us/insurance/
Wisconsin
http://oci.wi.gov/oci_home.htm
Wyoming http://insurance.state.wy.us

Federal government website
http://www.firstgov.gov

This is the official website of the U.S. government, and it's filled with information and resources. The section entitled "Laws and Regulations" contains links to searchable legal databases, a copy of the U.S. Constitution and other laws, information on how the court systems work, access to government publications and links to legal resources. That's only one segment of this extensive site. No subscription is required for this valuable resource – you've already paid for it with your tax dollars.

Bureau of Justice Statistics
http://www.ojp.usdoj.gov/bjs

This is the official website of the Bureau of Justice Statistics, the government agency responsible for compiling numbers about anything pertaining to criminal justice in the United States. The website contains information concerning criminal offenders, victims, law enforcement, prosecution, the federal court system, corrections, and other related topics.

Books

Law Dictionaries

You might want to have access to a legal dictionary when you're just starting your bail bond business. You can find and bookmark numerous free websites listing legal terms, or you might want a simple pocket dictionary. *Merriam-Webster's Dictionary of Law* is only $12 in paperback, or *Dictionary of Legal Terms: A Simplified Guide to the Language of Law* by Steven H. Gifis is $9 in paperback.

If you're more serious about law, you can pick up *Black's Law Dictionary*, edited by Bryan Garner. This reference book is more detailed and includes the U.S. Constitution. Its $60 in hardcover, $25 in paperback.

Criminal Justice Guides

For a thorough academic view of our criminal justice system, try *Introduction to Criminal Justice*, 9th edition, by Joseph J. Senna. This detailed textbook explores the history, procedures, ethics, theories, vocabulary and other aspects of our criminal justice system. It's $75 in hardcover.

If you just want the basics, try *Law 101: Everything You Need to Know About the American Legal System* by Jay M. Feinman. It's only $20 in hardcover, and it covers the Constitution, civil law and procedure, contract and property law, criminal law and criminal procedure.

Accounting references

You might want to learn the basics of accounting to do the bookkeeping for your bail bond agency. Try *Accounting for Dummies* by John A. Tracy (a *For Dummies* publication) or *Small Business Accounting Simplified* by Daniel Sitarz (Nova Publishing). Both paperbacks sell for approximately $16 and are written for individuals with no formal background in accounting.

INDEX

ABOUT THE AUTHOR

Sean M. Cook has been in the bail bond business for over 12 years. While working for one of the largest bail companies in California, he gained extensive knowledge of the industry. A few years later, Sean ventured on to open his own bail agency, which he has operated for the past decade. Since then, he has acquired another bail agency and has the largest bail online presence with his website http://www.Bail.com. Sean is considered a bail bond expert among bail professionals. He wrote this book to fill a void in the industry about bail bonds, how they work, and how someone can go about setting up a successful bail bond company. Sean lives in California.

BAIL BONDS 101

"This book is a must have. It explains in detail the workings of the bail bond industry. I recommend it to all of our bail agents, whether they are seasoned veterans or new bail agency owners or managers. This book is great for the industry!"

Scott Anschultz
American Contractors Indemnity Company

"This book gave me the information I needed to start my business. I am now running a successful bail bond practice in Nevada. Without Sean Cook's guidance and knowledge of the business, I wouldn't have felt as comfortable starting my bail bond agency. Thanks to Sean Cook for his hard work writing this book."

Chad Reichle
Chad's Bail Bonds

"I have worked with Sean Cook for several years now. He has proven to be a professional in the industry. He continues to pave the way, setting new standards of excellence. His book is one of a kind. The information in this book is vital to the running of a successful bail bond business."

Eduardo Almeida
National Bonding, Florida